REVERSALS OF FORTUNE

Why has history so often turned the economic and political hierarchy of nations topsy-turvy? This book examines the evidence of the last 500 years to challenge the two dominant narratives on the answers to this question. It argues that the explanation lies neither in the quality of institutions that societies possess nor in their capacities for technological innovation. What matters for the economic and political success of a country, it claims, is the interaction between current technological knowledge and global demand on the one hand and its geography and the population it inherits from its past on the other. Those societies succeed whose endowments best fit the requirements of current technology and world demand. It hardly matters who developed the technology.

In the process of examining the patterns that inform the fates of nations over time, *Reversals of Fortune* charts the economic histories of Western Europe and Asia from the sixteenth century to the present day.

A compelling *tour de force*, this book reshapes and rethinks global history. The volume will be a fascinating read for scholars of history and economics, especially economic history and human geography.

Ashok Sanjay Guha is Professor Emeritus at the School of International Studies, Jawaharlal Nehru University, India. He has also taught at Yale, the University of California (Berkeley), UCLA, Syracuse University, the University of Colorado, the University of Melbourne and the Institute of Development Studies, Sussex. He has been a consultant to the World Bank, the Planning Commission, the Ministries of Finance and Commerce, Government of India, the University Grants Commission, the Union Public Service Commission, the Indian Council of Social Science Research and the All India Council of Technical Education. In 1982, he was awarded the VKRV Rao Prize for outstanding contribution by an Indian economist.

A few of his recent publications include the volumes *Economics without Tears: A New Approach to an Old Discipline* (2017), *Markets and Morals: Some Ethical Issues in Economics* (2011) and many pieces in major international scholarly journals and Indian newspapers.

REVERSALS OF FORTUNE

Why the Hierarchy of Nations So Often Turns Topsy-Turvy

Ashok Sanjay Guha

LONDON AND NEW YORK

First published 2021
by Routledge
2 Park Square, Milton Park, Abingdon, Oxon OX14 4RN

and by Routledge
52 Vanderbilt Avenue, New York, NY 10017

Routledge is an imprint of the Taylor & Francis Group, an informa business

© 2021 Ashok Sanjay Guha

The right of Ashok Sanjay Guha to be identified as author of this work
has been asserted by him in accordance with sections 77 and 78 of the
Copyright, Designs and Patents Act 1988.

All rights reserved. No part of this book may be reprinted or reproduced or
utilised in any form or by any electronic, mechanical, or other means, now
known or hereafter invented, including photocopying and recording, or in
any information storage or retrieval system, without permission in writing
from the publishers.

Trademark notice: Product or corporate names may be trademarks or
registered trademarks, and are used only for identification and explanation
without intent to infringe.

British Library Cataloguing-in-Publication Data
A catalogue record for this book is available from the British Library

Library of Congress Cataloging-in-Publication Data
A catalog record for this book has been requested

ISBN: 978-0-367-81943-9 (hbk)
ISBN: 978-0-367-46604-6 (pbk)
ISBN: 978-1-003-02989-2 (ebk)

Typeset in Bembo
by Apex CoVantage, LLC

CONTENTS

Preface		*vii*
1	The problem	1
2	The mysteries of technological progress	10
3	Ocean navigation and the grand reversal	23
4	A short note on New World reversals	49
5	The first industrial nation and its many reversals of fortune	56
6	Full circle	75
	Epilogue	96
References		*100*
Index		*105*

PREFACE

Fluctuations in the balance of power and wealth between countries and regions have been the stuff of international politics and matters of endless interest in economics for ages. As a teacher of students of economics as well as of international politics, I have been bombarded throughout my career with questions seeking explanations of such fluctuations. This book is my attempt at answering some of them. My first and most important debt is therefore to my students.

In figuring out my answers, I have profited immensely from the work of great thinkers who have trodden the same path before me, Geoffrey Parker, Carlo Cipolla, Douglas North, Eric Jones, Acemoglu, Johnson and Robinson, Joel Mokyr, Deirdre McCloskey, Robert Allen, Jared Diamond, Kenneth Pomeranz, Jeffrey Williamson and innumerable others. My debt to them is enormous, though my explanation differs from theirs.

I must also acknowledge the kindness of the editors of *Revista di Storia Economica* in permitting me to base parts of a chapter of the book closely on a joint paper by Brishti and me, published in that journal in 2014. I am equally grateful to the editors of the volume *Planning and Economic Policy in India* (Manabendu Chattopadhyay, Pradeep Maiti and Mihir Rakshit) and to Sage Publications India for permission to reproduce extracts from my paper in that volume in Chapter 6 of this book.

On a more personal level, I owe much to my daughter, Brishti, who not only co-authored with me a paper on which Chapter 3 of this book is based but helped me throughout with critical comments and suggestions at every step. Her patience and encouragement and that of my wife, Indrani, made the writing of this book possible.

1
THE PROBLEM

I met a traveller from an antique land,
Who said – "Two vast and trunkless legs of stone
Stand in the desert. . . . Near them, on the sand,
Half sunk a shattered visage lies, whose frown,
And wrinkled lip, and sneer of cold command,
Tell that its sculptor well those passions read
Which yet survive, stamped on these lifeless things,
The hand that mocked them, and the heart that fed;
And on the pedestal, these words appear:
'My name is Ozymandias, King of Kings;
Look on my Works, ye Mighty, and despair!'
Nothing beside remains. Round the decay
Of that colossal Wreck, boundless and bare
The lone and level sands stretch far away."
– P. B. Shelley, "Ozymandias"

Reversals of fortune

History is replete with examples of forgotten empires, of the flowering of splendid civilizations and their decay, of the rise of states and economies to greatness and their often catastrophic collapse. Perhaps the most dramatic and critical historical event of the last millennium was the fall of the Asian empires that dominated the world until the seventeenth century and their replacement by the hegemony of Atlantic Europe and America. What accounts for this momentous reversal of fortune? And what lessons does it hold for present and future generations? These are questions that have long engaged social scientists of all varieties – historians, political scientists, sociologists and, inevitably, economists.

2 The problem

As is just as inevitable, when economists jump into the fray, controversy erupts and clouds issues, in particular the issue of whether there was actually a 'reversal' or only a rapid widening of a possibly pre-existing but narrower gap, a 'great divergence'. For economists, this is a question that can be resolved only by a comparison of living standards or per capita GDP of the Asian and European worlds in the sixteenth and seventeenth centuries. Given the scarcity, or rather the absence, of data, such a comparison is fraught with heroic assumptions and cavalier interpretations. If we permit ourselves such liberties with data, the balance of opinion would probably be slightly in favour of 'divergence' rather than 'reversal'. However, somewhat more reliable estimates exist of population densities (which presumably indicate the capacities of different economies to support life) and urbanization (which reflects the food surplus generated by agriculture). And calculations based on these lend more support to the reversal hypothesis than to the notion of a mere divergence.

Perhaps this is one of those issues that are too arcane to be irrefutably resolved. However, there can be little doubt that, until the seventeenth century, the Ming and Manchu empires of China, the Mughals of India, the Safavids of Iran and the Ottomans of Turkey surpassed any European monarchy in power, magnificence and influence on the world order. Yet by the mid-nineteenth century, the rise of Europe and its pioneering role in global economic growth had turned the pecking order of the nations of the world completely on its head.

But the 'European miracle' and its corollary, the Asian eclipse, are far from being the only examples of the world's balance of power turning topsy-turvy. Embedded within the European story are many similar, though smaller, stories. The Mediterranean countries, especially Italy, the fifteenth century centre of the Renaissance, the home of Galileo, Leonardo, Michelangelo and the Medicis of Florence, fell in the late sixteenth and seventeenth centuries into precipitous decline as the Atlantic efflorescence began. On the Atlantic shores of Europe, the Iberian countries, the fifteenth- and sixteenth-century pioneers in ocean navigation, declined in the seventeenth century to the status of minor powers even as their Northern neighbours, England, France and Holland, flourished. Holland, the economic powerhouse of Europe during the Dutch 'Golden Century', the seventeenth, faded away in the eighteenth on the eve of England's Industrial Revolution. England, workshop of the world until the late nineteenth century, surrendered its industrial leadership soon after to the great continental economies of the United States, Germany and Russia.

This tale of explosive growth in one region matching inexorable decline in another continues to be repeated today. Since the 1970s, the advanced West and Japan have fallen into near-chronic depression with real wages stagnant in the United States and employment contracting in Europe while East Asia and, since the 1990s, South Asia as well, have grown at rates unprecedented in human history.

Is this continuous alternation in global economic leadership, this rise and fall of countries and regions over the long run, a random process, driven by chance events and factors? Or is there an underlying pattern to which it conforms?

Acemoglu, Johnson and Robinson on the reversal

In a classic and justly celebrated series of papers at the beginning of the present millennium, Acemoglu, Johnson and Robinson[1] (AJR) argued that such a pattern can indeed be discerned in the success-and-failure stories of the world economy over the last 500 years. They claimed that there has been a systematic reversal of fortune between the successful economies of 1500 and the laggards by the end of the twentieth century and that this reversal of fortune was driven by differences in institutions between these two groups of countries. The institutional differences were in turn the product and legacy of different patterns of European colonization. According to AJR, Western Europe pioneered the development of a set of institutions that fostered free markets and property rights and thereby facilitated rapid growth. During the era of colonial expansion which began in the sixteenth century and accelerated over the next 300 years, Europeans transplanted these institutions in some of their colonies but not in others. In countries where they settled, primarily the 'neo-Europes', the United States, Canada, Australia and New Zealand, they imported the institutions to which they were accustomed at home, institutions that favoured economic development. In contrast, in countries in which they ruled but did not permanently live, they aimed to get rich quick by establishing and exploiting extractive institutions which not only militated against long-run growth but tended in fact to reduce these economies to penury. In any country, long-term European settlement was favoured by a congenial and healthy climate and, to a lesser extent, by the availability of free land. In regions of high mortality and dense populations, Europeans did not settle: they preferred to loot and to create institutions that facilitated plunder. These were the disease-ridden tropics and the densely populated countries that had been wealthy before the advent of Europe. The extractive institutions created by the colonialists outlasted colonialism; they were inherited and used by the native elites that succeeded, so that their adverse impact on growth was perpetuated.

AJR establish their hypothesis through an elaborate set of econometric exercises. They demonstrate that investors' estimates of the risk of expropriation in a wide cross-section of countries correlate negatively with the 1995 per capita incomes of these countries. They believe that expropriation risk is a summary negative measure of institutional quality: it reflects the unfriendliness of local institutions to economic development. Not surprisingly, this may have an adverse impact on economic performance. However, statistical association of the two does not establish which is the cause and which the effect. Poor economic performance may well have given rise to a hostility to free markets reflected in investors' perceptions of high expropriation risk.

To establish the direction of causation, AJR set up a more controversial econometric exercise. They construct measures of white settler mortality for each country during the early phases of colonial expansion using a variety of rather dubious data sets. They then show that these measures of settler mortality in the distant past are negatively related to the per capita incomes of the

4 The problem

respective countries in 1995. Reverse causation – from low per capita income today to high settler mortality in the past – is hardly plausible here. The channel of direct causation that AJR explore is the one charted out previously: high settler mortality was, very credibly, a strong deterrent to white settlement in the disease-ridden regions. This created a bias in white colonial policy towards get-rich-quick enterprises and extractive institutions and policies. Institutional inertia then guaranteed that the successor states in the colonial countries retained the same extractive character.

The moral that AJR wish to convey is that the secret of economic growth lies in the quality of institutions, specifically in institutions that foster economic freedom. Western Europe created such institutions early, then exported them to the settler colonies of 'neo-Europe' but not to the rest of the world. This is what explains the existing distribution of world income and the reversal of fortune that the successful economies of earlier eras have suffered. But before we accept their message, we should perhaps examine their proof a little more closely. One could, of course, begin by questioning their data, particularly their rather idiosyncratic construction of past settler mortality.[2] However, their method raises issues that are far more important than their data. AJR observe an association between their construction of settler mortality rates in the past and the current economic performance of many countries. The link between the two, according to them, lies in the institutions that resulted from these mortality rates. They do consider some other possible links but observe that their inclusion does not improve the fit. They infer that institutions, and institutions alone, contain the basic mechanics of economic development.

AJR's method is akin to the technique of elimination sometimes used in whodunits to identify the culprit responsible for the body in the library. As all readers of crime fiction know, this is a method with the widest possible margins of error. We may believe we have spotted the murderer by ruling out all other possible suspects – but a closer look may well reveal the prodigal son just back from a long exile or the butler concealing his ample proportions behind the library curtains. In the case investigated by AJR, there is no shortage of missing butlers or prodigal sons. To cite just one example, an obvious link between past settler mortality and current economic performance, a link that owes nothing to institutional quality, is the malaria parasite.[3] Malaria was the prime killer of white men in the tropics before quinine. It is still the scourge of Africa and parts of South and East Asia, reducing labour productivity and per capita income, if not killing people outright. AJR's proof fails the 'exclusion test', the requirement that it exclude all variables that might conceivably explain both settler mortality and current economic performance independently of institutions.

Further, if AJR are not just telling a story that applies only to their chosen endpoint of 1995 but are designing a more general recipe for successful growth, their results have to hold even when endpoints are shifted. Their conclusions should be able to withstand a 'robustness check'. But if AJR were to terminate their exercise not in 1995 but in 1850, they would discover that the most successful economies at that point of history were the Caribbean countries and the Southern states of the United States, buoyed by thriving plantations of sugar, cotton and tobacco and luring capital and, despite their unhealthy climates, immigrants as well from Europe and the less privileged North East and Midwest of the United States. They would find also that the institution that was the key to the success of these economies was not economic freedom at all, but slavery.

If AJR were to project current economic trends into the future and extrapolate their exercise, say, to 2050, they would almost certainly find that the most successful economies at their new endpoint were East Asian and perhaps South Asian, with Australia possibly thrown in. With this partial reversion to the sixteenth-century economic hierarchy of nations, what lessons could one draw about the institutional bases of economic growth?

In fact, a major problem with the AJR scenario is that it models economic growth as a linear process: countries with good institutions succeed, those without fail. There is no place in the story for a once-successful economy to falter and fail – unless, of course, some extraneous intervention – foreign conquest perhaps – destroys the pre-existing good institutions and replaces them by bad ones. Yet in point of historical fact, such stories are legion. Even within the 'European miracle', the declines of Italy, Spain, the Netherlands or twentieth-century Britain indicate that, despite supposedly good institutions, growth is often reversible or at least self limiting.

This is not to suggest that institutions do not matter. Quite the contrary. Security of property and contracts is indispensable for economic transactions of any kind since no one will buy what the seller doesn't own or cannot be relied upon to deliver – and without transactions, economic life itself is impossible, leave aside economic growth. Security requires a military, policing and judicial apparatus which must be operated and funded by a coercive institution, the state. The financial requirements of this apparatus can be met either by arbitrary expropriation or by a regular and predictable tax system. The coercive apparatus must enforce a body of law that is impersonal, predictable and calculable, so that people can figure out the consequences of their actions. All these institutions – and many others – are essential for the functioning of any economy, and their quality is obviously critical for economic success.

However, there are at least two reasons one may dispute the primacy of institutions as determinants of economic growth. First, institutions may assume a variety of very different forms. Even as basic an institution as the state may sometimes be replaced by substitutes without major economic damage. History provides examples of subeconomies that developed and indeed flourished for long periods in the interstices between different political jurisdictions on the basis of their own unique institutional arrangements. The Maghrebi traders' coalition, a group of Jewish merchants based in North West Africa, traded all over the Mediterranean between the eleventh and thirteenth centuries without any legal protection whatsoever in the Muslim and Christian countries where they functioned.[4] The Champagne fairs were the main forums of international trade in medieval Europe for hundreds of

6 The problem

years. Yet the merchants at the fairs came from many different countries with no common legal or judicial apparatus to decide their disputes and without the Champagne authorities having any coercive power over them.[5]

Secondly and more importantly, institutions, unlike geography, are not carved in stone. Nor are they the products of random events that, through the institutions they give rise to, leave their imprints on history forever. Institutions evolve under the pressure of a variety of forces, and it is difficult to assert that they are prime movers rather than adaptations to possibly more basic factors. The direction of causality is often impossible to establish; the exclusion test – which AJR fail so conspicuously – is often an unsurpassable obstacle to an econometric resolution of the question.

Alternative explanations: technology?

But if we reject the AJR model, what explanation can we offer for the patterns of rise and fall of economies worldwide which is the stuff of our story? A belief popular in an age of spectacular scientific and technological achievement is that innovation is the key to economic growth. And certainly major surges of global growth have typically been associated with key innovations. Here is a sample.

1   Open-ocean navigation – the technology of steering a course at sea with no landmarks visible – led to the Commercial Revolution, the great expansion of maritime transport and trade from the sixteenth to the eighteenth centuries that powered the rise of Europe and the discovery and settlement of the New World.

2   The smelting of iron ore by coke – rather than by coal or charcoal – together with the invention – or rather the reinvention – of the steam engine in the eighteenth century laid the basis for the Industrial Revolution. They liberated economic activity from its thraldom to human and animal sources of energy and its dependence on organic materials by harnessing fossil fuels and metals locked up hitherto in the bowels of the earth, thus transforming the world from the late eighteenth century onward.

3   Railways, developed in the 1820s, powered the opening up of the interiors of great landmasses in the United States, Canada, Australia, Germany and Russia with their rich agricultural and mineral resources and revived Western Europe from the Ricardian-Malthusian food crisis it faced in the 1830s and 1840s. The process was further accelerated by the invention of the internal combustion engine.

4   Turn back the pages of history to the discovery of the techniques of navigation in landlocked seas, the consequent flowering of the Mediterranean civilization and the rise of the states of Greece and of the Roman empire. Or peer into the even more distant past when the technology of river navigation and of large-scale irrigation led to the rise of the river valley civilizations in the basins of the Hwang Ho, the Indus, the Nile and the Tigris-Euphrates.

MIT Nobel Laureate Robert Solow, in one of the most widely cited papers of all time, provided empirical support for the view that technical progress is the mainspring of economic growth.[6] He assumed constant returns to scale. On this premise, he calculated that, over the first half of the twentieth century, less than half of the rise in US output could be explained by the increase in factors of production like capital and labour. The remainder – the so-called Solow residual – he attributed to technical progress.

Solow's exercise, like all novel ideas in economics, evoked a measure of dissent. Solow did not allow for the improvement in the quality of labour due to education and resulting higher skills and thus underestimated the contribution of labour to economic growth. His assumption of constant returns to scale ignored the role of scale economies in key twentieth-century US industries like automobiles and steel. It also neglected the benefits of the growth of trade as transport costs fell, permitting a finer division of labour and the exploitation of the comparative advantage of different regions as well as of the US economy as a whole. Thus, benefits accessible within the existing technology were included within the Solow residual and wrongly counted as technical change. Despite these limitations, Solow's conclusions resonated so strongly with the twentieth-century cult of science and technology that they continued to dominate thinking on economic development.

Since Solow's seminal paper, the triumphal march of science and technology has only accelerated. Over the last fifty years, science has unlocked for us the secrets of the atom. It has cracked the genetic code and transported us into outer space and the wonderland of instant long-distance communication and remote control. Thanks to it, we have conjured up life in the laboratory and acquired the capacity for its total and immediate annihilation. Since the sixties, science has transformed our consumption patterns; our ways of life and our technologies of production, transport and communication. The momentum of economic growth worldwide has accelerated to a pace undreamt-of in earlier eras. The nerve centre of this massive scientific and technological revolution has undoubtedly been the United States, followed at some distance by Western Europe. And yet . . .

And yet, the regional pattern of economic growth has been very different from that of technical progress. During the space age and the biogenetic and IT revolutions, the high-tech West has stagnated, while East Asia has enjoyed astronomical growth, a process to which, as the economists Alwyn Young[7] and Lawrence Lau[8] have irrefutably demonstrated, technological progress has contributed little or nothing. The Pacific Miracle has been a triumph of relatively low technology. So too over the last twenty-five years has been the rapid economic growth of abysmally low-tech South Asia. Here is one of the major paradoxes of contemporary economic growth.

Nor is this mismatch between scientific and technological leadership and rapid economic growth a recent aberration. Spain and Portugal pioneered the technology of open-ocean navigation in the late fifteenth and the sixteenth centuries. Spanish expeditions discovered America, penetrated Central and South America and discovered the Pacific. Portuguese explorers rounded the Cape of Good Hope, discovered

8 The problem

the sea route to the East and circumnavigated the globe. In the process, the Iberians invented or improved the basic techniques and instruments of ocean navigation and accumulated information about coastlines and harbours, winds and currents that was indispensable to later seamen. They mastered the methods and the weaponry of open-ocean warfare and designed the ships that were optimal for it. Yet the long-run beneficiaries of their technology were the maritime countries of North West Europe, England, France and Holland. By the seventeenth century, the Iberians had been relegated to the status of minor powers while England and Holland ruled the seas, with France not so far behind.

The railway locomotive was invented in England in the 1820s by George Stephenson. But the prime beneficiaries were great continental countries like the United States, Canada, Germany and Russia, countries that, by the end of the nineteenth century, had ended England's ascendancy as 'the workshop of the world', the world's greatest industrial power.

Johannes Gutenberg invented the printing press in Mainz in 1440. But the printing revolution that followed – with its corollaries of mass communication and literacy – spread explosively beyond the limits of Germany to the far corners of Europe. By 1480, printers were at work in 110 different places in Germany, Italy, France, Spain, England, Switzerland, Poland, Holland and elsewhere; by the end of the century, printing was well established in more than 400 European cities.

In more recent times, the invention of the modern internal combustion engine by Nicolaus Otto in Germany has not constrained its geographic diffusion worldwide. Nor did the conceptualization of the modern programmable computer by Englishman Alan Turing in the 1940s give England a marked advantage in the subsequent history of the computer industry.

Why does scientific and technological progress on the most spectacular scale – whatever its impact on the global economy as a whole – not translate into economic acceleration in the country where it actually originates? Why, during the most brilliant half-century of its scientific accomplishments, has the West languished in economic stagnation? This is a mystery to which there have been few answers, and one which we try to unravel in the next chapter on technology.

But if neither institutions nor technology hold the key to the economic success of a country or region, what does? Geography, one would assume, must play a part, since growth – or decline – often occurs not in isolated economies but in geographically well-defined clusters. We find the Mediterranean world prospering in one period or the North Atlantic coast or East Asia. Large river valleys flourish in one age, maritime economies in another, great continental hinterlands in a third. AJR, of course, are emphatic that geography has nothing to do with it (except for its role in determining early settler mortality). They show that distance from the equator or from the coast, rainfall, mineral wealth or a variety of other geographical advantages (or disadvantages), taken by themselves, are uncorrelated with the distribution of world economic growth. And, indeed, this is hardly surprising. What was a geographic advantage in one age may cease to be one in another: an extensive ocean coastline is of no value if the technology of open-ocean navigation is unknown;

fertile virgin land or rich inland mineral deposits do not constitute an asset unless means of easy access exist. The value of a country's geographic endowment depends on how well it fits into the current pattern of world trade and technology. And we suggest that it is the interaction of geography with technology and trade that determines the pattern and distribution of economic growth.

Unlike geography, however, technology is not an exogenous factor in the growth process. New technology does not descend like manna from heaven: it is an outcome of growth as well as a trigger of further change. There is a complex process of interaction in which geography shapes the consequences of a new technology for the distribution of income within and between countries, but this in turn determines the pattern and tempo of further innovation. So, while we reject the theory that technology is the recipe for the economic development of any country, we must begin our search for the mainspring of growth by looking closely at the economics of technical change, both its causes and its consequences. This is what we propose to do in our next chapter.

Notes

1 D. Acemoglu, S. Johnson, J. A. Robinson, The Colonial Origins of Comparative Development: An Empirical Investigation, *American Economic Review*, 91, 2001, pp. 1369–1401.

D. Acemoglu, S. Johnson, J. A. Robinson, Reversal of Fortune: Geography and Institutions in the Making of the Modern World Income Distribution, *The Quarterly Journal of Economics*, 117 (4), 2002, pp. 1231–1294.

D. Acemoglu, S. Johnson, J. A. Robinson, Institutions as a Fundamental Cause of Long-Run Economic Development, in *Handbook of Economic Growth*, 2005.

2 AJR have no direct evidence of past white settler mortality but construct the variable on the basis of fragmentary unrelated data such as the death rates of Catholic bishops in hot and cool regions, of white soldiers in war and peace and of African labourers.

3 See J. Sachs, Government, Geography and Growth, *Foreign Affairs*, September–October 2012.

4 A. Greif, Contract Enforceability and Economic Institutions in Early Trade: The Maghribi Traders' Coalition, *American Economic Review*, 83 (3), 1993, pp. 525–548.

5 B. Guha, Who Will Monitor the Monitors; Informal Law Enforcement and Collusion at Champagne, *Journal of Economic Behaviour and Organization*, 83 (2), 2012, pp. 261–277.

6 R. M. Solow, Technical Change and the Aggregate Production Function, *Review of Economics and Statistics*, 39 (3), 1957, pp. 312–320.

7 A. Young, The Tyranny of Numbers: Confronting the Statistical Realities of the East Asian Growth Experience, *The Quarterly Journal of Economics*, 110, 1995, pp. 641–680.

8 L. Lau, J. Il Kim, The Sources of Economic Growth in the Newly Industrialized Countries on the Pacific Rim, in L. R. Klein, C.-T. Yu (eds.), *The Economic Development of ROC and the Pacific Rim in the 1990s and Beyond*, 1994.

2

THE MYSTERIES OF TECHNOLOGICAL PROGRESS

The strange history of innovations

Some time probably in the sixth century BCE, an Indian physician named Sushruta wrote a medical text, the Sushruta Samhita, which described, among other medical marvels, the technique for reconstructing a severed nose, a technique that, in its essentials, is still in use by plastic surgeons today. In the next two millennia, the book was buried in libraries (though translated into Arabic in the eleventh century CE), and the method passed into oblivion except for a family of potters among whom it was orally transmitted from generation to generation as a rather unimportant trade secret. Only in the 1790s did two English surgeons witness a successful rhinoplasty performed in the manner of Sushruta by a Madras potter and break the news to an incredulous West.[1]

Shift focus to a different continent and a different age, Roman Alexandria in the middle of the first century CE. A Greek engineer, appropriately named Hero, has developed the world's first steam engine. At the great temple of Alexandria, once a sacrifice is offered at the altar and the holy fire lit, the thermal energy generated is used by the engine to automatically open the doors of the temple. The assembled host of worshippers is thunder-struck: the gods have opened the doors themselves and entered to accept the offerings at the altar.[2] Yet nothing further is heard of the steam engine until over 1600 years later, when Thomas Newcomen reinvents it for the very mundane purpose of draining water out of mines. For this vast intervening span of time, the key invention of the Industrial Revolution lies in total oblivion.

Much better known than either of these episodes is the affair of Leonardo da Vinci's notebooks. In these, that genius of Renaissance Italy describes in detail designs for a flying machine, a helicopter, a tank, a diving bell and a variety of other devices that were fated not to become realities for another 500 years. Meanwhile, all this technology, painstakingly mirror-written from left to right, survived only in collectors' archives to stir the imaginations of scientists the world over.[3]

These three examples illustrate first that technological progress is very far from an exponential, or a linear or even a unidirectional process; the pace of accumulation of knowledge is very uneven; nor is knowledge always added: it is often forgotten or lost. Second, the growth of technology is not closely correlated with that of science. As in the case of the modern steam engine, an understanding of the basic scientific principles may precede their effective application to technology by millennia – so that technological innovation is rarely guided by 'the inner logic of scientific knowledge'.

Yet innovations occur when the time is ripe . . .

On the other hand, most innovations are not random processes – Alexander Fleming's chance discovery of penicillin through a laboratory accident notwithstanding. Never-ending lists can be compiled of simultaneous independent inventions or even of multiple simultaneous discoveries of scientific principles. For a small sample of multiple inventions, consider the following. The telegraph was invented independently in 1834 by Wheatstone in England and Morse in the United States. The Bessemer process for steel was developed in 1851 by American William Kelly and independently in 1855 by Englishman Henry Bessemer, who patented it. In 1876, Elisha Grey and Alexander Graham Bell filed patents for the telephone independently but on the very same day. In 1879, the Englishman Swan and the American Edison independently developed the incandescent light bulb. The Hall-Heroult process for the extraction of aluminium was independently developed in 1886 by the American engineer Hall and the French scientist Heroult. Among major scientific methods or principles, the best-known examples are the simultaneous discovery of calculus by Newton and Leibnitz and of evolution by natural selection by Darwin and Wallace. Much less provocative of controversy were Mendeleev's construction of the periodic table of elements in 1869 and Julius Lothar Meyer's independent publication of it in 1870. Likewise, in 1905, Nettie Stevens of Bryn Mawr and E. B. Wilson of Columbia peacefully but independently traced sex differences to differences in sex chromosomal endowment – the fact that men have XY and women have XX sex chromosomes. In fact, one could multiply examples indefinitely.

Multiple independent inventions suggest that innovations occur when the time is ripe for them. This could, of course, reflect the logic of the gradual accumulation of scientific knowledge, as claimed by Robert Merton[4] and suggested by Newton's famous and uncharacteristically modest attribution of his success to the fact that he was 'standing on the shoulders of giants'. Indeed, no innovation is possible unless the essential infrastructure of scientific knowledge is already in existence. However, the examples I have cited at the beginning of this chapter suggest that this is far from sufficient. Innovations occur when societies urgently require solutions to specific problems. This is the factor that affects the incentives of scientists and inventors: it focuses their attention in particular directions by promising rewards in terms of money and fame.

12 The mysteries of technological progress

A striking example of the link between the key problems faced by a society and the innovations it generates relates to the development of perhaps the purest of the pure sciences. Astronomy was long believed to be the province of the proverbial absent-minded scientist secluded from worldly concerns in his ivory tower, the star-gazer. Yet the chronology of the explosive rise of modern astronomy, of the work of Copernicus, Kepler, Galileo, Tycho Brahe, which changed forever our view of man and the universe, cannot possibly be explained without reference to the major economic and technological problem that confronted Europe in the late fifteenth and sixteenth centuries. This was the problem of open-ocean navigation, of the transition from an economy based on the land-locked Mediterranean to one that faced outward to the Atlantic. Steering a course on the open ocean without visible landmarks for guidance required celestial navigation and the most intensive and accurate knowledge of the stars and their motions, knowledge far beyond what Aristotle or Ptolemy could offer or the Vatican sanction. Indeed, there are records of prizes being offered by the British Crown, by the States General of Holland, by Philip II of Spain and Louis XIV of France for the best method of determining longitude at sea, a competition in which Galileo himself participated.

And where they are needed

It was not only the rise of new scientific disciplines that reflected urgent contemporary economic problems. The general character of technical inventions was also largely determined by existing resource scarcities. The eighteenth century, when British textile producers found themselves unable to compete with the low-wage cotton spinners and weavers of Bengal, opened the floodgates for the deluge of labour-saving inventions in the cotton textile industry that is often described as the starting point of the Industrial Revolution. The late nineteenth and early twentieth centuries, when American wages were the highest in the world, also saw the United States becoming the world's major centre of labour-saving invention. Due to its high density of population on usable land and its location in an earthquake zone which inhibits high-rise construction, Japan faces perhaps the most acute scarcity of space in the world: it is also the world leader in miniaturization, in space-saving innovations, ranging from *bonsai* to micro-electronics.

A possible way of visualizing the innovation process is in terms of the gradual discovery of an array of potential new products and processes lying just beyond the horizon of preexisting technology. The inventor seeks to tap into the latent demand for these goods and techniques that, at the moment, exist only in the imagination. The stronger this potential demand, the more urgent will be his search, the larger the effort and resources he will devote to it.

In the realm of consumer goods, the demand for new products arises typically from the upper reaches of the income distribution. Before the unification of the world market, this was essentially a demand for exotica: it arose largely due to the demonstration effect of different consumption patterns from foreign parts and was fulfilled by imports from them. For the European consumer, silk, tea and porcelain from China; muslins from India; spices from India and Indonesia; chocolate and tobacco from America; and sugar from tropical plantations worldwide all fitted into this story. These were the staples of the medieval luxury trade along the silk road and the spice route and the trans-Atlantic trade of the seventeenth and eighteenth centuries. But with the globalization of the world economy, imports were no longer considered unfamiliar, and the taste for novelty could only be satisfied by imagining and conjuring up brand-new products unknown anywhere earlier. The demand for novelties is necessarily strongest at the higher income levels since the rich have already experienced and explored the more familiar products. And at the early experimental stages of a new product, close interaction is needed between the laboratory, the shop floor and the market to discover and iron out any glitches in product design or production technique. This ensures that development and production of brand-new consumer goods are typically attracted to the richest economies.

For producer goods and intermediates, demand for innovations arose at pressure points of the existing technology where shortages of key resources emerged to raise costs. In coal-mining, for example, the exhaustion of the shallower seams forced a deepening of mines to levels at which the existing air pumps could no longer pump the subsoil water out of the mine. This led to a search for a more powerful source of energy that culminated in Thomas Newcomen's development of the steam engine. Likewise, charcoal smelting of iron ore led to deforestation and a scarcity of timber that motivated Abraham Darby's discovery of coke-smelting.

Innovations and potential profitability

These macroeconomic impressions are strongly confirmed by microeconometric studies of the behaviour of firms. The empirical work of Griliches,[5] Mansfield,[6] Scherer[7] and Schmookler[8] establishes the correlation of technical progress with profit considerations determined by economic needs. Schmookler, for instance, shows that the number of patents taken out by a firm (which is a reasonable proxy for its rate of innovation) is proportional to its sales volume. This implies the Adam Smith–like proposition that the rate of technical progress is limited by the size of the market – a proposition with a highly plausible economic rationale: the larger the market for an industry, the higher the returns on the research cost of an invention relating to it, the stronger therefore the incentive to innovate.

While the rate of innovation reflects the size of the market, its direction is largely determined by resource scarcities. Labour-saving innovation, for example, adds more to profits the higher the share of labour in total costs: in other words, it will be more profitable when wages are high and labour is relatively irreplaceable within the pre-existing technology. Allen, in fact, has developed a whole theory of divergence on the basis of this notion of *biased* technical progress.[9] Consider an economy in which, for whatever reason, wages are high relative to prices of other inputs. If there are no good substitutes for labour within the current technology, labour-saving innovation will be induced. This will increase labour productivity, wages and per capita income. The higher wage will reinforce the incentive for further labour-saving

14 The mysteries of technological progress

technical progress, and so on in a cumulative process. The low-wage economy, meanwhile, will not find it profitable to develop or adopt the labour-saving technology and will therefore be left behind. Allen's model requires the assumption of a highly elastic product market. If labour productivity rises but product demand does not, unemployment will emerge and drive wages down, aborting the cumulative process. Nor will Allen's model be relevant in a neo-classical world where free trade and capital movement equalize factor prices internationally, the kind of world which perhaps we are gradually approaching (and which is outlined in Chapter 6). Whatever the merits of Allen's theory of divergence, the importance of factor prices in shaping the character of technical progress is undeniable.

These two factors – the level of demand for a product and the scarcity of those of its inputs which have no good substitutes – together set the rate and pattern of profit-driven technical innovation.

Other sources of innovation

Of course, not all technical progress is profit driven. New technology has three possible sources. It may be begged, borrowed or stolen from other societies. It may be the costless by-product of what Kenneth Arrow called 'learning by doing': as one accumulates more production experience, tinkering with processes and machines, possible improvements occur to one and add to productivity. Or technology may progress as a result of investment of time and resources in research.

Demand and innovation

However, whether it is the product of technology piracy or lease, learning by doing or investment in research, technical progress is associated with high levels of demand. This is what makes expenditure on leasing, piracy or research worthwhile, while the pace of learning by doing is related to how much one does – that is, to the actual volume of production (and therefore of demand). Of course, there is a difference in principle between the two: learning by doing is a function of actual production, while investment in research reflects its anticipated level. But since expectations are generally based on past and present experience, the two are pretty difficult to disentangle empirically: if technical progress is faster in a large market, is it because that provides more opportunities for learning by doing or because the expectation that large demand will persist in future stimulates more investment in research? Possibly, it doesn't matter.

Thus, whether innovation results from technology piracy, from investment in research or from learning by doing, it is associated with large sales volumes. How would an inventor or his patron achieve or protect the large sales volume that is the basis of his invention? In a static economy, he may be spurred by the prospect of reducing costs to break into a large profitable monopoly or of deterring potential rivals from invading a monopoly of his own. Portugal's exploration of the sea route around Africa is said to have been motivated by the urge to outflank the Moroccan monopoly of the trans-Saharan trade in gold and slaves and the Venetian monopoly of the spice trade with the East through Egypt. The extraordinary innovativeness of US firms today amidst general economic stagnation has been attributed to their need to survive in a Schumpeterian world of competing oligopolies where the development of new products is almost the only industry in which the United States has not priced itself out of the world market.[10]

An additional incentive for technical progress exists when overall demand is itself expanding and one producer need not encroach on the territory of others to increase sales. Growth of demand, once it begins, tends to generate its own momentum. As demand increases and output responds, savings and investment rise, adding to capital, output, income and more demand. However, in an inquiry into the *origins* of growth, one needs to look at the exogenous forces that could initiate the process even when the starting point is a state of stagnation. In a closed economy, like the earth as a whole, the main factor of this kind is population pressure on resources. This could be the outcome either of resource depletion or of population growth. Population pressure works both through the market and the political process to stimulate development and technical progress. On the one hand, it initially changes the pattern of private consumption (as distinct from its level), leading to increased demand for food, clothing and shelter. Given the difference in input requirements, these demands cannot be fully met at unchanged prices by simply diverting resources released by contracting sectors. Scarcities therefore emerge, prices rise, and innovations are eventually induced, thus ultimately increasing income and effective demand. On the other hand, population growth depresses standards of living (at least until it induces technological progress); it thereby generates discontent and pressures for government action to increase income. Ester Boserup has suggested that the major innovations in the history of agriculture were consequences rather than causes of population growth,[11] an opinion that has been widely criticized, more on grounds of logic than of fact. The mechanism we have described provides some analytical justification for the Boserup thesis.

In an economy open to external influences, there are at least three other sources of growth: military competition with rival societies; earning opportunities abroad through trade, investment or indeed plunder; and the demonstration effects of advanced patterns of consumption elsewhere.

The inflow of income from abroad, of profits, remittances and booty, and the multiplier effects of its re-spending on domestic demand are of course familiar themes that have been intensively explored.

The demonstration effect of new goods and ways of life operates, like population growth, on two levels. It generates discontent and demands for higher incomes that force governments down the path of development through increased demand. It also motivates individuals to work harder, save and invest more, take more risks and experiment with newer technologies, thus enhancing output and income in order to increase their ability to buy the new goods. The two effects complement each other.

16 The mysteries of technological progress

Finally, armament in response to increased military pressure directly increases the demand for public goods. It stimulates research for a superior technology of war and better logistics of communication and supply – affecting demands throughout the country. In many senses, this is the most compelling factor of all, since the survival of the state, perhaps even the society itself, is put at stake.

Innovations, then, typically emerge when there is a large or growing demand for a product or service in highly inelastic supply both at home and abroad. The large demand was perhaps being catered to earlier by a profitable monopoly that the innovator wishes to invade. Or perhaps a growth of aggregate demand has created markets that never existed earlier. Had supplies been scarce domestically but elastic abroad, this would have resulted only in the growth of imports. But if imports are inelastic as well, we have the classic situation of necessity being the mother of invention. Of course, the infrastructure of knowledge must already be in existence; otherwise, an innovation may require too great a technological leap to be possible.

The constraints on private research and innovation

Further, there exist major barriers to research-induced innovation. These arise from the characteristics of the product as well as the process of research activity. The product of research – technical knowledge – is such that its description, characteristics and value cannot possibly be assessed in advance of production. Thus research is surrounded by uncertainty – and this uncertainty cannot be insured against because of moral hazard – the possibility that insurance will induce the researcher to slack off.

A second characteristic of technology is its essentially public good character, a point that we elaborate later. The cost of reproduction of much technical knowledge is negligible compared to its cost of production, and in most societies, restriction of access is difficult and costly. Research in a market economy is therefore constrained by the fact that its product is only very imperfectly appropriable.

On the other hand, technology that *can* be appropriated through trade secrets or effective patenting pre-empts competing research: it inflicts losses on those who have lost the race, losses that are not internalized by the pioneer who chanced upon the solution first. Thus research that does not generate external economies produces external diseconomies. These reduce the average and increase the dispersion of profit rates on research.

The characteristics of research as a production process are as distinctive as those of technology as a product. It is subject to strong economies of scale to be realized through team-work because of the spreading of fixed costs, the non-duplication of effort and the cross-fertilization of ideas. Further, research activity is extremely difficult to monitor: inputs of research activity are not commensurable directly, nor can they be readily assessed because of the uncertain character of the fruits of research and the impossibility of isolating the contribution of any individual to a team effort.

This complex of characteristics tends to depress incentives for individual research. The high degree of risk and the missing markets for insurance (on account of moral hazard) discourage the risk-averse but otherwise inventive individual. Economies of scale coupled with absent or imperfect capital markets for the financing of research (moral hazard again!) prevent the entry of aspiring inventors who lack capital. The pre-emption effect reduces the average profitability and increases the riskiness of research. The difficulty of monitoring individual effort creates acute moral hazard in collective or corporate research ventures and deters investment in them.

Finally and most importantly, the non-appropriability of much knowledge deters private research. Knowledge, unlike material assets, cannot readily be turned into private property. The cost of excluding trespassers is simply too high. In earlier ages, the diffusion of knowledge could be controlled only by treating it as a family secret, perhaps orally transmitted from generation to generation with strict injunctions against disclosure to any outsider. Trade secrets, on the other hand, could be readily breached: one could always lure away the knowledgeable person if, as Henry Ford famously announced, every man has his price. Inventions could always be begged, borrowed, bought or stolen. In consequence, they either became common knowledge freely available to everybody or ended up in the hands of those who stood to gain the most from their application and were willing therefore to spend the most on acquiring them. Intellectual property rights, beginning with the patent acts, have slowed down this process of diffusion but are far from extinguishing it. Discoveries cannot be patented, nor can scientific principles. Patents themselves have a limited life-span and can always be 'invented around'. Mansfield, Schwartz and Wagner,[12] in a survey of 100 leading US firms, found that 'information about the detailed nature and operation of a new product or process generally leaks out in about a year'. In consequence, the private returns from innovation are often far too meagre to induce the costly research that it may require. The inventor often needs a patron, at least in the early experimental stages of his work.

Innovation and the state

Private research is not therefore a very inviting field of activity. Most basic research requires patronage: it has to be funded or underwritten by a larger entity which can internalize at least some of the externalities it generates, perhaps in fact by the state. This has its costs – the moral hazard of the researcher is greatly intensified by state financial support, but there often is no other option. Certainly, there was hardly any alternative to state subsidy in the age before global IPR protection. The fate of basic innovations in that era reflected the incentive of the state to subsidize them. The state subsidized innovations that promised a substantial revenue yield or increased the income and importance of the ruling elite. It suppressed innovations that threatened to reduce these or to increase the power and wealth of rival groups. Typically, the incumbent groups in a state are the beneficiaries of the preexisting technology and are therefore averse to its replacement by a new one. States, then, have a conservative effect on technology and a retarding influence on growth. However, sometimes the ruling elite is itself divided and a faction, perhaps even the dominant faction, may support the new technology. This is more likely to happen

18 The mysteries of technological progress

when the old technology has exhausted its possibilities and is running into diminishing returns. When it does, the state may well become the major patron of the new technology.

Of course, the state is always the key force behind technical change in the field of military technology. This is an area in which no patents are respected and each technological leader has to protect its own secrets. It is also an area in which states are least reluctant to spend since the continuance of the incumbent depends on it and one in which societies are most easily persuaded to authorize spending on the plea, occasionally true, that the barbarians at the gates are preparing to erect mountains of civilian skeletons unless repulsed. Military innovations funded by the state have extensive spin-offs in civilian technology. Examples are legion. They range from nuclear power and medicine, jet engines, air traffic control systems and microwave ovens (which are by-products of radar), laser technology (which owes its present incarnation to Reagan's Star Wars initiative), programmable computers (first developed in the Ballistic Research Laboratory of the US Department of Defence), the internet (pioneered by the Department of Defence's ARPANET Project in the 1960s), satellite communication and navigation and digital photography (all of which originated in the spycams used in the space race) to many far more mundane applications. Duct tape was originally developed as a means of waterproof sealing of ammunition cases. Aviator sunglasses had been designed long before Tom Cruise as a means of protecting the eyes of fighter pilots from ultraviolet radiation. Canned food and freeze-drying technology were originally intended to serve the nutritional needs of soldiers on the front line. Scientific disciplines like meteorology, oceanography, seismology and geodesics owe many of their current content and techniques to defence research.

Military investment, research and innovation are guided by threat perceptions. From what quarter does the threat arise? How powerful is it? How technologically sophisticated? These are the questions that determine the intensity and direction of a country's military research and innovation. A continental empire with an open land border will be primarily interested in the technology of land warfare, especially when the threat of inroads from across the frontier is acute. An island kingdom will focus on navigation and the technology of marine warfare. A state with long boundaries, both on land and at sea, may have to face a dual threat and a consequently unbearable strain on its resources or choose to concentrate on the one frontier that it perceives to be critical.

The perceptions of the state are of course coloured both by history and by the interests of its dominant groups. And history and the status of the elite both reflect the pre-existing technology. Great land empires are associated through both cause and effect with an overwhelmingly land-oriented technology and a landed elite with a stake in this technology. They are also likely to have had a long history of invasive pressures and border conflicts across their land borders. This is the quarter from which they expected major threats to arrive, the frontier they believed they must defend at all costs and the direction to which their military investments and innovations would therefore be oriented. For them, the sea and the coast were but a secondary source of revenue, merchants and mariners lacked affluence and political influence and the threat from the ocean, so the imperial regime believed, could not possibly penetrate its inland core.

In contemporary times, military technology has become so generalized that the role of geography in shaping its orientation has dwindled. We are entering the age of remote-controlled warfare based on drones, robots, satellite-based intelligence and guidance devices to ensure precise targeting and computerized command and control systems. Military technology of this variety reaches well beyond the constraints of geography both in its applicability and its threat potential. But it is so costly and technologically so sophisticated as to be out of reach of all countries except those with the very highest economic and technological capacity. *Innovations at the cutting edge of military technology are the preserve of a very few countries and are no longer shaped by national geography.* However, military *investments* continue to be determined largely by geography, by vulnerable borders and spaces and proximate enemies.

Conclusion

To recapitulate, innovations require a large potential market which cannot be served within the existing technology due to supply inelasticities. Most basic innovations, those that generate major external economies by creating a new technological paradigm or opening up a new economic frontier, also need intellectual property rights protection. When this is inadequate, as it was before the modern era, they require state support, at least in their early experimental stage. Well-established and highly successful states, however, were often disinclined to provide such support since they were dominated by elites that had prospered under the pre-existing technology and were therefore committed to it. Less successful states and societies, those that had not adapted quite so perfectly to the older technology, would have been more supportive of innovation that could create opportunities hitherto unexplored.

However, the public good character of knowledge has one major consequence. It implies that the geographic locus of an innovation – the question of where it originated – has relatively little to do with who will be its major ultimate beneficiaries. Its economic impact is largely a matter of location theory, not a question of provenance: how does it affect the profitability of different locations, not where was it invented? The locational effect of an innovation has three aspects, none of which are necessarily tied to its country of origin. Its *primary* effect arises through its requirement of conditions or inputs that are bound to the country in which it is deployed. The fifteenth- and sixteenth-century innovations in maritime transport and the discovery of new ocean routes were largely the product of Spanish and Portuguese effort. But the prime beneficiaries were countries with a high ratio of coastline to surface area and good harbours well connected with their hinterlands, such as England, Holland and France. George Stephenson invented the railway locomotive in England in the 1820s, but large continental landmasses with vast cultivable land areas and mineral resources like the United States, Canada, Russia and

20 The mysteries of technological progress

Germany reaped the bulk of the fruits. England no doubt flourished as a result of Abraham Darby's invention of coke-smelting of iron, Thomas Newcomen's steam engine and James Watt's condenser. But this was less due to their being Englishmen (Watt was in fact Scottish) than to the geographical fact that readily accessible and abundant reserves of coal and iron ore existed in England in close proximity. Indeed, in the long run, Pittsburgh and the Ruhr owed just as much as the British Midlands did to these three gentlemen and to their successors in steel-making, such as that other Englishman, Sir Henry Bessemer. The personal computer, the internet and the mobile phone, whatever their origins, have revolutionized ways of living and of doing business the world over.

These are but a few examples of how innovations have a *direct* impact on people and production quite remote from the countries where they were developed. But they also have substantial *indirect* effects similarly distant from their places of birth. A *secondary* effect arises through the demand that the innovation creates for inputs that are scarce in the country where it was invented or the ones where it is applied on a large scale but are both freely available elsewhere and highly mobile. The revolution in textile technology that vastly expanded the scale of cotton textile production totally transformed parts of the world best suited for cotton plantations. The internal combustion engine changed the economic structure and prospects of countries with huge oil reserves. Sometimes several innovations worked together to generate a demand for an input that could be supplied by a specific region far away from the sites where these innovations were developed or applied. The late nineteenth-century explosion in the demand for automobile and bicycle tyres, for industrial gaskets and for insulated electric and telegraph wires sustained a huge demand for rubber that resulted in large-scale rubber plantations in Malaya, Indonesia and Sri Lanka.

An even more remote consequence of innovation, a *tertiary* effect, could be triggered by the changes it induces in the prices of internationally immobile factors in the country in which it is introduced. If it raises the price of one factor (say, labour), it raises the cost in that country of other goods that use that factor intensively (labour-intensive goods) and their prices. It thereby attracts labour-intensive imports from low-wage countries and may even impel migration of capital to these countries to finance labour-intensive production. Much of the economic history of the last fifty years can be explained in terms of the growth of the production and export of manufactures from labour-abundant Asian countries exploiting the differential between their wages and those of the high-tech Western world.

The long-run consequences of innovation are thus independent of its source, even though the pioneer may derive some immediate advantages from *seignorage* – the right of first use – before the innovation becomes common knowledge or is otherwise acquired by his competitors. What matters ultimately is the closeness of fit between an innovation and the environment of the country we are considering. Some features of the environment can, of course, be adapted to the requirements of a new technology, and some aspects of a technology can be modified to suit a new

The mysteries of technological progress **21**

milieu. There are, however, other characteristics of a country that are immutable, and the central profile of a technology cannot generally be changed. How well do the two match?

It is this that determines the extent to which a country benefits from an innovation. The most basic immutable characteristic of a country is its geography, and it is the interaction between geography and technology that largely shapes the relative long-run growth prospects of different countries, whatever the origin of the new technology. A new technology empowers and accelerates growth in countries that most closely fit its requirements and is likely to be adopted most rapidly by such countries. If, as is likely, radical departures in technology have radically different geographical requirements, reversals of fortune are the inevitable outcome.

Geography summarizes the unchanging natural differences between countries. There are, however, other man-made devices that artificially sustain and perpetuate differences that may have otherwise disappeared over the course of time. By far the most important of these are migration restrictions. Successful economies tend to acquire and nurture large populations. Once their heyday passes, excessive numbers become a drag on their development but cannot be exported to other economies that are presently at the forefront of the world economy because of limited labour mobility. Some of this immobility is a matter of transport cost and disappears as technology improves – as in the case of the nineteenth-century migrations from Europe to the New World. Much of it, however, is due to migration restrictions. These result in long-run international differences in capital/labour and man/land ratios and correspondingly in wage rates and per capita incomes. Innovations that change the importance of labour costs in production therefore have dramatic effects on the relative economic performance of different countries in a system of sovereign states insulated behind immigration barriers.

A final question: what kinds of innovation are crucial in economic history? Obviously, the larger the scale on which an innovation is deployed, the wider will be its repercussions. Innovations in the fields of food production, transport and energy have the most pervasive effects. We focus on changes in transport technology as the crucial initiating factor in the geographical shifts in economic leadership that are our main concern. However, as we shall see, innovations in agriculture and energy use also had key geographical effects which cannot possibly be ignored.

Notes

1 For a fuller account, see B. Guha, Ancient Wisdom, *The Telegraph*, February 17, 2015.
2 See J. Mokyr, *Twenty-Five Centuries of Technological Change*, London: Routledge, 2001.
3 See F. Capra, *Learning from Leonardo*, 2013.
4 J. G. Leyburn, On the Shoulders of Giants: A Shandean Postscript by Robert K. Merton, *Social Forces*, 44 (4), 1966, pp. 603–604.
5 Z. Griliches, D. Jorgenson, The Explanation of Productivity Change, *Review of Economic Studies*, 34 (3), 1967, pp. 249–283.
6 E. Mansfield, *Industrial Research and Technological Change*, New York: W. W. Norton, 1968.
7 F. M. Scherer, Firm Size, Market Structure, Opportunity and the Output of Patented Inventions, *American Economic Review*, 55 (5), 1965, pp. 1097–1125.

22 The mysteries of technological progress

8 J. Schmookler, *Invention and Economic Growth*, Cambridge, MA: Harvard University Press, 1960.
9 R. C. Allen, Technology and the Great Divergence: Global Economic Inequality since 1820, *Explorations in Economic History*, 49, 2012, pp. 1–16.
10 W. J. Baumol, *The Free Market Innovation Machine*, Princeton: Princeton University Press, 2002.
11 E. Boserup, *The Conditions of Agricultural Growth*, London: Allen and Unwin, 1965.
12 E. Mansfield, M. Schwartz, S. Wagner, Imitation Costs and Patents: An Empirical Study, *Economic Journal*, 91 (364), 1981, pp. 907–918.

3

OCEAN NAVIGATION AND THE GRAND REVERSAL[1]

The starting point of this book, as of many others, is the most important reversal of fortune in the history of the last millennium, the eclipse of the Asian empires and their replacement by the dominance of the Atlantic West between the seventeenth and nineteenth centuries. The present chapter examines the story of this prolonged but dramatic change. In particular, we seek to interpret this transformation in the light of the interaction between geography and technology, which, we believe, is the key to an understanding of the regional pattern of long-term economic growth.

The central theme of our story is the rise of open-ocean navigation and its impact on the balance of power and prosperity between the continental and maritime regions of the world. The new technology of transport created new opportunities for trade, extending markets that fostered the growth of industries and towns in locations best placed to exploit it. It also stimulated the development of new weaponry and military tactics as new theatres of war opened up along the new trade routes, and these military innovations and the associated technological capability enabled those who acquired them to conquer and dominate those who did not.

Ocean navigation fitted the geography of maritime Europe, and the returns it promised offered Europeans the incentive to invest in the risky enterprise of its early development. For any individual pioneer, however, this incentive was attenuated. The information he discovered at much cost, about winds, currents and coastlines; about methods of steering in open oceans and about the optimal design of ships and their armament, all rapidly and inevitably became common knowledge to be readily exploited by his rivals. At least in the early experimental phases of his ventures, the true pioneer needed the support of his state if he was to create this 'public good'. And his state would subsidize him if and only if this was in the interest of the ruling elite. A secure, well-established ruling elite, however, typically reflected the pre-existing

24 Ocean navigation and the grand reversal

balance of power based on an older technology. As the prime beneficiary of the older technology, it had little interest in its replacement by a new one. In the great continental empires of Asia, dominated by a landed elite based on agriculture, land transport and land warfare, state support for risky maritime experiments was highly improbable. In the mercantile republics of the Mediterranean, which had flourished on the basis of navigation in landlocked waters, in Genoa and especially in Venice, there was so little interest in the open ocean that the Genoese Christopher Columbus had to resort to Ferdinand and Isabella of Spain for patronage of his venture into the unknown West. Things were very different in Atlantic Europe. There, engagement with the sea was a geographic necessity even in the age of land transport. It could sustain, therefore, a maritime interest with a financial and political potential that was not altogether a negligible rival of the landed interest. The political elite was divided and state support for Atlantic ventures a distinct possibility. This, of course, is the story of the Atlantic explorations of Portugal and Spain.

After the state-supported great leap into the unknown by the Iberian pioneers, a host of North West European imitators swarmed in. Their adaptations and minor extensions of the knowledge of ocean transport acquired by the Portuguese and the Spaniards required and received less government help. However, state support was indispensable for one aspect of their commercial operations – the military. The states of Britain, Holland and France had every incentive to support their traders militarily and did so with gusto.

In contrast, the great Asian empires not only failed to generate the seminal innovations in maritime transport and warfare technology but also did nothing to encourage their subsequent acquisition. China, in fact, went to considerable pains to destroy the not-insignificant marine capability it had earlier developed. The Asian states remained absorbed in their continental preoccupations, in their agriculture and land revenue and in the defence of their land borders against continental invaders. Thus it was that by the mid-eighteenth century, North West Europe captured the seas of Asia virtually unchallenged, her trade and, eventually, by the nineteenth century, much of her land.

Once Europe's political dominance was established, the policies of Asian states reflected the interests of the European metropolis, not those of the Asian economies. This was the major proximate cause of the stagnation or retrogression of Asia from the eighteenth century to the mid-twentieth, precisely in the era of the economic transformation of the Atlantic West. In this sense, the reversal of fortune was indeed an institutional phenomenon. It was driven by the failure of Asian institutions, primarily political institutions, to adapt to the requirements of modern economic growth. But the causes of this failure – and of Europe's success as well – lay deeper – in the differences in the relative match between geography and transport technology in the two regions. Asian states, institutional structures and military methods reflected the continental character of Asia's geography and were highly successful in an earlier medieval era dominated by land transport. In the new age of ocean navigation, they were obsolete. Europe's geography and her experience were just the opposite – and it was this oppositeness that lay at the root of the reversal of fortune.

The economic geography of medieval transport

Our story begins, therefore, with transport technology in the Middle Ages and its impact on the economics and politics of medieval Eurasia. The geography of Eurasia is in turn central to the characteristics and evolution of medieval transport. From East to West, Eurasia consists of the coasts and archipelagos of Pacific Asia, the river valleys of the Hwang Ho, the Yangtse, the Mekong, the Ganga, the Indus, the Tigris-Euphrates, the Arabian desert, the landlocked Mediterranean and Atlantic-facing peninsular Europe – all surrounding an immense continental heartland. But, blocking the main East-West sea routes of Eurasia lies the impenetrable African landmass. Not only does this compel a vast detour but also – because of the off-shore trade winds down the West coast of the Sahara – tends to deflect all shipping way out into the Atlantic.[2] Up to the fifteenth century, therefore, Eurasian maritime transport moved in two separate orbits: (1) the European orbit centred on the landlocked Mediterranean and (2) the Indian Ocean orbit from the Red Sea and the Persian Gulf to the South China Sea, an orbit dominated by the monsoon. The technology of navigation and of naval warfare in each circuit suited the specialized requirements of the Mediterranean on one hand and the Indian Ocean on the other. The discontinuity between the two circuits meant that seafaring methods which were of value mainly in the transition from one to the other were neglected. The technology of open-ocean navigation in the Atlantic was, of course, known. The Norse voyages of the High Middle Ages to Iceland and Greenland or Leif Ericsson's fabled journeys to Labrador would not have been possible without means of accurately determining position and steering a course on the high seas. But these voyages were too unrewarding to be pursued, and the techniques they involved fell into disuse and oblivion. The technology of open sea warfare, of guns and sails, of naval artillery and the naval architecture that went with it, was as yet in the future. Intercontinental trade was largely land bound. It followed the silk roads of Chinese Turkestan or the spice routes through the Persian Gulf and the Red Sea down to the caravan routes of the Middle East.

Land transport was costly. It was based on draft and pack animals: it required forage and fodder for animals on the move and was accordingly prohibitive in areas of settled agriculture. It was cheaper on the steppe, where animals could find free pasture as they travelled. Even so, costs were high and included protection costs that had to be paid to all rulers en route and the risks of drought and of brigandage were ever present. These costs were, in fact, highest on the steppe, with its mobile war-like population.

Indeed, the high costs of transport were so pervasive a feature of medieval life that in many senses, the Middle Ages can be best understood as the Age of Immobility.

The economics of the Age of Immobility

Prohibitive transport cost meant that medieval trade comprised essentially light high-value luxuries. It also limited trade volumes and therefore economies of scale and comparative advantage, thus curtailing income and driving up manufacturing

26 Ocean navigation and the grand reversal

cost. Demand for and output of most manufactures was restricted both by low income and high unit costs and prices. Production was overwhelmingly agricultural. Land, therefore, was the main source of revenue (supplemented by tariffs on the luxury trade, which also travelled primarily over land). Rich agricultural regions therefore became the centres of great states and magnets for invaders. Warfare, and therefore military technology, were essentially oriented towards the land. There was little interest in methods of maritime combat.

Land transport and medieval war: the basis of feudalism

Militarily, the high cost of transport made long-distance logistics inordinately expensive. The problem of supplying distant garrisons often decided the configuration of society and state. One possible solution was military decentralization. Specific pieces of land would then be defended on the basis of local resources alone. Where the military threat was essentially peripheral, the consequences would be frontier warrior colonies or frontier feudalism.[3] Where threats were more generally dispersed, the feudal mode of organization became universal. In regions facing a peripheral threat – but on a barren frontier – large-scale canals were constructed to move food from the fertile heartlands to the frontier garrisons. The standard example was the conveyance of supplies from the rich Yangtse provinces of Ming China along the Grand Canal to the Northern garrison defending Peking and the Great Wall.

Transport technology affected not just logistics but military operations as well. Land warfare with low-tech land transport meant that the horse was the primary military carrier. The mobility of a cavalry living off the land far outstripped the possibilities of food supply and economic integration between regions. Distant peoples interacted militarily, as predator and prey, more often than commercially. Security was a more compelling concern than affluence. Military capability was the main basis of political authority, with economic power relegated distinctly to the background.

The use of the horse for warfare followed two distinct lines.[4] The first involved light cavalry, essentially highly mobile mounted archers using the nomad tactics of rapid manoeuvring, ambush and surprise attack. Light cavalry reigned supreme right across the Eurasian steppe into North China and North Western India and across the Hungarian steppe to Vienna. But it could not penetrate the dense, humid forests of North and West Europe. It was restricted to the dry, open grasslands where the light horse mainly bred and where it could be optimally deployed.

This was also the happy hunting ground of the pastoral nomad – the tribesman for whom mobility *en masse* was a way of life. Here entire populations lived off the soil and on the move.

The peasantry of less arid regions lived quite differently. Mass mobility was impossible in agrarian economies; here large armies could not live off the soil. Such lands responded to the pressures of light cavalry using the bigger, stronger horses that could be bred on their richer pastures. The strength of these horses – and the innovation of the stirrup – made heavy armour for horse and rider possible. The armoured horseman and his mount were both costly and specialized. They implied a full-time warrior elite with each warrior supported by the surplus of a large agricultural territory. Transport cost made the collection and centralization of such a large surplus for the benefit of a central standing army prohibitive. So, the main elements of the army, the knights, were dispersed over the domain, each collecting and subsisting on the surplus of a specific piece of territory. The foundations of feudalism everywhere were military – in Sassanid Persia, in Byzantium with its cataphract-bowmen or in the Muslim Middle East where it was formalized under the Turks by Nizam-ul-Mulk. Of course, the feudal institutions were most fully developed in Western Europe: here the armoured knight with his lance effectively sustained the defence of Western Christendom.[5]

Transport and the regional balance of power in the medieval world

Insignificant sea trade and landlocked transport and military technologies skewed the regional balance of power. They favoured hinterlands over coasts, continental interiors over ocean margins, culminating in the dominance of the Central Asian steppe over Eurasia. The steppe's financial strength was based on the tribute it drew from intercontinental commerce – because of both its location and its free pasture, which depressed the costs of animal-based transport and so tended to attract trade.

The steppes were also the prime breeding grounds of the horse – the indispensable means of land warfare and rapid land transport. The horse trade was a flourishing line of commerce and a rich source of income to the steppe lords. The horse was also the basis of their military near-invincibility. Together with the locational advantage of the steppe and the mobile way of life of the steppe-nomad, the horse conferred on the steppes unique military advantages: forces could be massed and deployed at the right places and the right time, intelligence accumulated and effective control and command exercised over an area unequalled before modern times. Conquerors from the steppe could isolate and attack agricultural civilizations and maritime peoples. Thus, impulses from the steppe, waves of migration and conquest emanating from its interior dominated medieval history. They destroyed the classical world and moulded the age that followed. From the fall of Rome to the rise and evolution of feudalism in Europe, the erosion and eventual supersession of Arab hegemony by the Turks in West Asia, the chaotic fragmentation and eventual collapse of Hindu India and almost the entire dynastic history of China from the Yellow Emperor to the Manchus – this entire millennium or more of history is dominated by pressures from the steppe. It is the unifying thread in this chequered pattern.

The dominance of heartlands is manifest not only on the global but also on the national scale. Both in India and in China right up to the colonial era, the coasts were always subordinate to the interior – whether due to the rich agricultural

28 Ocean navigation and the grand reversal

resources of the latter or to its essential defensive functions ('strategic depth') in an age of land warfare.

The rule that coasts were not major sources of surplus did have its exceptions. Where the geography of transport dictated that a large volume of trade be funnelled through a single point, a port could become a highly lucrative asset. Examples include the Red Sea ports like Aden and Socotra; the Persian Gulf ports like Hormuz; Surat, Mamallapuram and Kaveripattinam in India; Malacca and the Chinese ports. But these Asian ports could never become independent centres of political power: they lived in the shadow of great land powers based in the fertile river valleys of Mesopotamia, India and China. Venice (and later Genoa) – situated at the crossroads of the trans-Alpine trade of Central Europe and the Mediterranean – could convert its commercial pre-eminence into political sovereignty because of its distance from any great natural centre of authority. Indeed, the geography of Europe – the absence of huge fertile agricultural areas like the Yangtse basin or the Ganga-Jumna doab, the peninsular character of the entire continent, and the diversity of climates (Mediterranean to temperate to Arctic) – soils, topography and mineral resources within a small area always tended to increase the importance of trade and of the sea relative to the land.

Transport and the rule of the nomad

Not only did the associated technologies of transport and war tilt the balance between regions in favour of the Central Asian steppe, they also selected between peoples. It made the horse-breeding steppe nomads the masters of Asia and of most of Europe from the Hungarian steppe Eastward.

The nomad's military advantages were many. His whole way of life was designed for mobility. His migratory habits, his tent-home, his mobile livestock property, the portability of his household goods – all minimized the costs of movement. Unlike the peasant rooted to the soil by his immovable property, his field, his farm, his terraces, his irrigation canals, the nomad was not committed to the defence of a fixed territory. He could withdraw his women and children, his herds and his home deep into the heart of the steppe, beyond the reach of the enemy, while enriching himself by raiding and plundering settled agriculturalists or townspeople.

The nomadic horseman's control of large herds of horses and his lifelong acquaintance with riding and horseback archery reinforced his mobility. Speed was a strategic and tactical weapon which he could exploit to a degree unequalled in the medieval world.

Finally, his means of livelihood and the geography of his homeland imposed on him a political structure and tradition ideal in many ways for the purposes of conquest. The herding instinct of horses ensures a high optimal ratio of livestock to labour in horse-breeding. And, given the medieval technologies of war and transport, the market for horses was lucrative. This facilitated the accumulation of vast horse herds and large fortunes among the horse-nomads, the emergence of an aristocracy and a well-developed social stratification. The horse-nomads, though tribal, had a high potential for internal political organization.[6]

Added to this were the geopolitics of Central Asia, particularly of Mongolia – the cradle of Central Asian state formation.[7] Here pressures from invading tribesmen from the Northern forests and the Han Chinese to the East converged on a grassland enclosed by desert and forest with only one Western outlet, the narrow Jungarian corridor. Here, enormous pressures could accumulate, and tribal warfare become endemic. Tribes would then disintegrate through dispersal or enslavement and free retainers cluster around chiefs, one of whom would eventually subdue his neighbours and found a state. Stratification rather than segmentation (as in a tribal society) would be the organizing principle. The states thus fashioned were conquest states. They were naturally selected by the circumstances of their birth for warfare. This was the political tradition that the Mongols and Turks inherited, and – combined with their way of life, their command over horses and their strategic location – it made them the conquerors of the medieval world.

The list of mighty Turko-Mongol conquerors and empire-builders is breathtaking. From Attila through Mehmud of Ghazni, Toghril Beg, Chenghiz Khan and his heirs and Timur the Lame to Akbar and Suleiman the Magnificent – it spans the entire course of medieval history. So does the long succession of Turko-Mongol dynasties. In China, the Khitan and the Kin rulers of Peking provided a foretaste of the Yuan century. In India, the Delhi sultanate was followed by the Moghuls. In the Middle East, the Seljuks, the Mamelukes and the Ottomans wrested control of Islam from the Arabs. Above all, there were the mighty empires of Inner Asia, culminating in that of the Chenghiz Khanite Mongols and their branches – the house of Kublai Khan in China, the house of Hulagu in Persia, the Golden Horde and the Mongol Khanates of Russia.[8]

The pressures built up among the nomads of the almost enclosed Mongolian steppe first hit the Great Wall and then, through the narrow Jungarian corridor, Turkestan and North Western Iran. From there, their impact reached India and the Middle East. But Northward, on the limitless expanse of the Russian steppe, the pressure was deflated: except in periods of extreme desiccation, the impetus for further nomadic advance into Western Europe was weak – at least compared to the devastating hordes that hurled themselves on North China and Persia. Further, it was not just remoteness and the buffer of the Russian steppe that protected Europe: it was her climate and vegetation. While North China, Iran and even North Western India were continuations of the semi-arid grasslands, Europe West of Hungary was humid and thickly forested. The marshes and forests of Western Europe impeded the mobility of the nomad's cavalry: it thereby tended to arrest the march of nomadic conquest.

Europe was thus less vulnerable to pressures from the Eurasian heartland than Asia. And, unlike Asia, it did not possess extensive sub-continental core areas of its own. Europe lacked the agricultural resources of vast alluvial plains on the scale of the Hwang-ho and the Yangtse valleys, the Ganga-Jamuna plain or even the Tigris-Euphrates basin. Its patches of fertile soil were separated by formidable natural barriers[9] so that its largest agricultural regions (the Loire Valley of France, for example) hardly compared even with the Kaveri valley core of the Chola empire.

30 Ocean navigation and the grand reversal

The agricultural hinterlands of Asia generated surpluses that sustained centralized states strong enough to dominate the coasts. But European kingdoms could never marshal resources on this scale from their interiors: central powers could not in consequence overshadow the European maritime periphery.

The European opening to the sea

The world of the Middle Ages faced landward. In economic and strategic dimensions, in class systems and the organization of production, in military technology and political structure, its concerns were continental. Geopolitically, Eurasia in the late Middle Ages consisted of three distinct components: (1) an inner core dominated by warlike horse-breeding nomads who exerted continuous pressure on (2) the agrarian civilizations of the Asian river valleys and (3) peninsular Europe, where smaller regional entities could live in relative immunity from the pressures from Inner Asia, though not from their own internecine conflicts. Each of these three constituents developed its own characteristic political structures: (1) the military empires of Inner Asia, based on land warfare and control of land trade routes; (2) the river valley empires of China, India and Mesopotamia, based on defence of a Northern frontier against nomads and the internal trade of a fertile agricultural plain; and (3) the European nation-state system comprising smaller monarchies without a rich agricultural base, compelled therefore to compete with each other to monopolize a potentially rich sea-trade.

While the conquest empires of the nomads had nothing to do with the sea at all, the alluvial empires flourished because of their rich agriculture and could survive only through effective defence of their Northern border against invasion. Their structure was determined by this prime function: they were dominated by warrior elites that controlled the central army and bureaucracies that collected the land revenue and used it to provision the army. Coasts and maritime trade were strictly secondary. Ports, merchants and naval concerns, while tolerated as long as they knew their places, could never be permitted to grow strong enough to disturb the internal balance of power. The strange Ming withdrawal from the sea after the age of the great voyages of Zheng He can, in fact, be explained by rivalry between the centre and the coast. An empire ruled from the interior did not want its coastal regions to prosper sufficiently to become rival sources of political power.

Unlike Asia, Europe West of the Elbe evolved political structures and traditions that were not entirely insensitive to pressures and opportunities arising from the sea. This reflected (1) its distance from and natural defences against nomadic invasion, (2) its lack of a rich agricultural base for a land empire and (3) its high proportion of coastline to land area. Thanks to the last factor, most of Western Europe was readily accessible from the sea, and maritime influences could penetrate more deeply inland and play a more significant role in the economics and politics of the continent. In particular, maritime trade and plunder could become important sources of funds and power and alternatives to land revenue as they never could have been in Asia. In Europe, they became major instruments in the hands of monarchs seeking to build nation-states out of feudal economies lorded over by local barons. During the recovery from the Black Death, in the late fourteenth and early fifteenth centuries, kings began successfully asserting their authority over feudal barons. Their capacity to do so was greatly enhanced by the import from China by way of the Mongols of gunpowder technology and the subsequent development of cannon, which made it possible for them to demolish the fortress-strongholds of feudal lords. And they found natural allies in a merchant class that resented feudal restrictions on internal trade and mobility. However, while the barons directly controlled the land revenue, the king needed an independent source of funds: he found this in maritime trade. Governments of fifteenth- and sixteenth-century European nation-states thus had a vested interest in ocean trade arising from the requirements of internal balance of power. The interests of the monarchical state and of maritime traders and pirates converged in a political alliance that deeply influenced the state's decisions about public investment.

The difference in geopolitical compulsions between the continents resulted in differential political structures. And it was this difference that helped explain the locus of transport innovation when it came and the very different responses that the innovation evoked.

The rise of open-ocean navigation and the discovery of the new sea routes were not random processes. They were the products of prolonged exploration and experiment. Much of the pioneering investment in the process was fruitless and most of it financially unprofitable. All of it would have been inconceivable without the strong support of states committed to the progress of seafaring. In Spain, in Holland, in England, and above all in Portugal, the state did develop such a commitment: political structures and tradition permitted and indeed encouraged it. But after the Ming withdrawal from the sea (see end notes 18 and 19 and the corresponding paragraphs), nothing of this kind emerged in the great empires of Asia. Some of them – like the Chinese or like Tokugawa Japan later – deliberately insulated themselves from maritime contact. Others tolerated navigation and trade, but their objectives were limited and specific – the Hajj pilgrimage, the import of war horses and the like; there was never the slightest semblance of any effort (apart from the early Ming voyages) to subsidize risky exploration or even technological improvement.

The greater interest of Europe in navigational methods and discovery was matched by – and indeed in part led to – her greater interest in the technology of naval warfare. In this, indeed, the influence of geography on the political structure of Europe acted as a stimulant. Europe emerged from the Middle Ages as a nascent states system – not as an empire or a set of empires. Its patches of fertile soil did not run together to form the core area of a large political unit but were divided by natural barriers that encouraged regional, rather than continental, entities. The consequence was intense political and military competition between the European states. With the rise of ocean navigation and trade, the arena of competition shifted out into the Atlantic. Guns were mounted on ships, and much effort was devoted to the adaptation of each to the specialized requirements of the other. Lighter, quicker-firing cannon were designed to replace massive bombards.[10]

32 Ocean navigation and the grand reversal

The technological basis was thus prepared for the evolution of the field-gun and the transformation of artillery from an instrument of siege warfare alone to a lethal and mobile weapon on sea or land. Meanwhile, the manoeuvrability and armament-carrying capacity of ships were vastly improved and the whole concept of naval warfare changed. Battles at sea were no longer decided by ramming and boarding but by manoeuvring and gunfire from a distance.

While the early development of naval artillery and the associated technology of ship-building and naval warfare occurred in Atlantic Europe generally, it is not surprising that it was carried to its logical culmination by England and Holland. These were the two states that had no commitment to the obsolete methods of Mediterranean navigation and warfare. By focusing on the new technology, the English and the Dutch rapidly acquired ascendancy over their Spanish, Portuguese, Italian and Turkish rivals, at least on the open ocean.[11]

The development of the field-gun in Europe lagged well behind that of naval artillery. According to Cipolla,[12] by the early sixteenth century, European naval bronze guns had been so perfected as to remain substantially unchanged until their displacement by cheaper iron guns more than 150 years later. 'Field artillery however remained the weak point of European munitions' until the Swedish innovations during the Thirty Years War. In the interim, it was the demand for naval ordnance that sustained European metallurgy, paving the way for the eventual transformation of the armaments and tactics of land warfare.

No such revolution in naval architecture or armament or in the technology of naval warfare occurred in Asia.[13] The Asian empires were basically uninterested in the sea, and on the few occasions when the imperial fleets took to the water, they faced but little competition on their limited courses. There was no real spur to improvement. Of course, when the Portuguese appeared in Asian waters, they swept all Asian fleets (except the Chinese coastguard) off the sea, but by then the technological lag of the others was far too wide, while the Chinese chose to cut themselves off from the mainstream of naval technology.

In the long run, indifference to the sea undermined Asian military effectiveness on land as well. Fire-power in Asia was never adapted to maritime use, so it did not pass through the essential experimental phase that led to the development of light mobile field artillery. Asian artillery continued to evolve in the direction of massiveness – appropriate for siege warfare – culminating in the monstrous artefacts of the Ottoman gunsmiths. Mobility was entirely sacrificed. The eventual consequence for Asia was an insurmountable handicap even in land warfare.[14] Thus, when the great empires decayed and the Europeans ventured forth from their coastal strongholds to challenge for supremacy on the mainland, they were militarily as irresistible as they had earlier been at sea. And Ottoman power, after its last thrust at the gates of Vienna in 1768, retreated Eastward in inexorable decline.

The Indian Ocean trade was, of course, first a segment of the expanding frontier of European navigation and commerce. There were the African trade, the Caribbean trade and the commerce of the American mainland. There was also the intensification of intra-European trade that stemmed from the technological revolution in navigation. All these areas offered European carriers the added advantage of relative proximity. So, once the Asian trade was captured, Europe had in effect completed the conquest of the whole world of maritime commerce.

It has sometimes been argued that the role of technology in this process is over-rated: freight costs on established trade routes did not drop significantly from the late Middle Ages until the nineteenth-century invention of the metal steam-ship.[15] Our primary concern, however, is not with improvements in sailing technology or ship design that cut costs on existing routes but with the opening up of entirely new routes and the revolution in naval (and, more generally, military) technology that enabled the West to control these routes and indeed all the oceans. O'Rourke and Williamson[16] have persuasively countered Lane's traditional thesis that Vasco da Gama did not matter, that the Portuguese voyages had little long-run effect on European markets. And while it is arguable that freight in (say) sugar or tobacco did not drop over very long periods, surely the fact that this trade existed at all only because of the discoveries is not a negligible consideration.

Atlantic Europe thus acquired its undisputed mastery over the seas of the world and over its trade. Both in the initiation of the new technology of transport and warfare and in its further development, she had advantages which she defended by force of arms to ensure her mercantile superiority. Once this was assured, there was less resistance to Asian ship-building and commerce, but by then the costs of developing the new labour skills and the fund of technical knowledge and trading contacts required for success in these fields was sufficiently daunting to deter all but the most foolhardy of potential Asian entrants.

An illustrative contrast: China and Portugal

Nowhere is the difference in compulsions and attitudes to the ocean of Asian and European states more vivid than in the contrast between mighty Ming China and little Portugal. The long land frontier of China proper, though protected to the West and South West by impenetrable mountains and deserts, lies open to the North. And no natural barriers intervene between this Northern border and the heartland of agricultural China. The North China plain and the fertile Yangtse basin are topographically continuous and indivisible and do not permit the maintenance anywhere of stable lines of internal defence.[17] Military equilibrium required a unitary authority over this vast region – an authority that could effectively defend the Northern border against the steppe nomads. Military security, and especially the defence of the Great Wall, was the prime function of the Chinese state. For two millennia, it maintained unchanged an institutional structure based on the interlocking of a Northern garrison that defended the Great Wall and a bureaucracy that collected the agricultural surpluses of the Yangtse provinces and conveyed them to the Northern army. The maritime trade of the Pacific provinces was never a focus of imperial concern.

One period represented an exception to this rule. This was the era of the Southern Sung (1127–1279), when the Han Chinese rulers had been driven South of the

34 Ocean navigation and the grand reversal

Yangtse by the pressure of the Jurchen tribes. Deprived *per force* of their obsession with the Northern land border, the Sung created China's first standing navy, a fleet of 20 squadrons totalling 52,000 men,[18] on ships armed with trebuchet catapults hurling gunpowder bombs and powered by paddle wheels. They developed a variety of nautical innovations, from watertight bulkhead compartments to an improved mariner's compass. They protected sea trade with South East Asia and fostered relations with South Eastern Asian powers. The Yuan dynasty (1279–1368), like the Sung, had no concerns about the Northern frontier – though for an entirely different reason. As part of the Mongol empire that stretched right across Inner Asia, it had no need to protect the North and no compulsion therefore to divert resources from maritime use for this purpose.

But with the return of the empire to its Northern borders, the Northern obsession and landward orientation of policy returned in full force. Chinese geopolitics after the Sung was typified by the Ming regime. As long as the Northern garrison had to be provisioned by sea from the Yangtse provinces, the Ming maintained an active interest in maritime trade and navigation, culminating in the seven great voyages of the eunuch-admiral Zheng He. In 1405, the emperor Yongle commissioned his follower, this faithful giant of a man, reportedly seven feet tall and almost as broad, to lead an exploratory voyage to the South China Sea, the Indian Ocean and the lands bordering them. Zheng He assembled an armada of 317 ships, some of them supposedly 120 metres long, the largest ever to take the water before the age of iron steam ships, with a crew of 28,000 and set sail on the first of his seven fabled expeditions. Over the course of the next twenty-eight years, he ensured effective Chinese control over South East Asian waters and the sea lanes across the Indian Ocean around Sri Lanka to Calicut on the Malabar coast. Across this vast area of ocean, he established a Pax Sinica, suppressing the pirates ensconced in Sumatra and defeating and capturing the refractory Sinhalese prince Avalokeshvara. Mostly, of course, it was sheer awe at the display of Chinese naval might that ensured tranquillity without military action. In his last three voyages, Zheng He reached across the Arabian Sea, not only to Surat in Gujrat but also to the Persian Gulf and Red Sea ports of Socotra, Hormuz and Aden and to the East African coast, to Mogadishu and Malindi. A flourishing maritime economy emerged in the region, providing China not only with zoological curiosa like ostriches, camels and giraffes but also with rare woods, ingredients for perfumery, dyestuffs, vast quantities of pepper and mineral inputs for pottery and absorbing the traditional Chinese exports of silk, porcelain and precious metals. Zheng He's well-documented feats – even if one dismisses as hyperbolical the reported dimensions of his ships or indeed his own dimensions – demonstrated the technological sophistication already achieved by China in ship-building, cartography, navigation and naval armament.[19]

But in 1435, the Grand Canal was completed. The defenders of the Great Wall could now be supplied by barge without resort to the riskier sea route, and Ming China withdrew landwards behind a barrier of official bans on maritime activity. The records of Zheng He's voyages were destroyed, so effectively indeed that our knowledge about him derives essentially from outside China, from Sri Lanka and

South East Asia, where he was revered and almost deified by the Chinese diaspora. The mighty navy was gradually dismantled, coastal settlement prohibited, foreign travel and contact with foreigners proscribed and sea-going vessels burned with so much fervour that a bureaucrat could boast that 'not an inch of plank now floats on the China Sea'. In the process, the Ming state not only withdrew its support to maritime enterprise, it actively did its level best to discourage and deter private maritime trade and ship-building. The fund of nautical knowledge and skill built up by the Southern Sung and augmented by the Great Voyages fell into disuse and oblivion. By the time that the Portuguese appeared in Asian waters, the great Chinese war-junks of Zheng He were a distant and fast-fading memory.

There can be no sharper contrast to late fifteenth-century China than the pioneer of the new technology of open-ocean navigation – little Portugal, hitherto a neglected backwater of the Mediterranean economy. Portugal's pioneering role was based on her location. She – along with Spain – represented the Mediterranean world's window on the Atlantic. She could tap Mediterranean sea-faring lore, the nautical skills and ship-building technology of Genoa and Venice. But she also knew the ocean and commanded – especially after the capture of Ceuta from the Moors (1415) – the West African coastal route, the obvious springboard for Atlantic exploration and commerce with its rich trade in gold and slaves.

However, the geographic compulsions that turned Portugal seaward extended beyond location. The rugged landscape of Portugal, her rocky soils and scanty irregular rainfall restricted cereal cultivation to a few fortunate plains like the fertile populous Northern province of Mino. Elsewhere, its extension depended on government investment in irrigation, which was very expensive on account of the violent fluctuations in river levels – perhaps the greatest in the world. But Portugal's Mediterranean climate sustained orchards and vineyards from which came citrus fruit, oil and wine, and the forests that draped her otherwise forbidding landscape yielded cork, wax and honey. Together with the coastal fisheries, these supported a range of specialized products that could profitably exchange for grain imports from North Africa. Thus, an urban mercantile class interested in trade and ship-building existed – though the backwardness of inland transport confined its activities to the coast – especially to Lisbon and Oporto.

Portugal was thus uniquely destined by nature for her pioneering role in the Age of Discovery. Her incremental comparative advantage lay in Atlantic trade and exploration. This was what promised the highest social returns on investment. But since the knowledge generated by the voyages was a 'public good', since it benefited later seafarers without the pioneer being able to capture a private return on these benefits, private individuals were necessarily deterred from pioneering ventures. Central to Portugal's overseas ventures, therefore, was the royal patronage of the House of Aviz. From the reign of Dom Joao I (1385–1433), and especially from the capture of Ceuta, the Portuguese Crown encouraged, financed and often organized the commercial, exploratory and colonial ventures of the Portuguese overseas, starting with the initiatives of Henry the Navigator. The Portuguese moreover were always keenly conscious of the externalities arising from these ventures: they sought

36 Ocean navigation and the grand reversal

to wrap their voyages and the information they generated in a veil of secrecy away from the prying eyes of alien seamen.

The government's policy of encouraging maritime enterprise followed the dictates of comparative advantage. But it also buttressed the authority structure. The feudal aristocracy – the owners of the large latifundia – constituted the main challenge to central authority, and, indeed, in the rebellion of 1383–1385 and the associated Castilian invasions, most of them had sided with the invaders. Extension of irrigated agriculture would have enhanced the power of potential dissenters. Maritime activity, the alternative channel of public investment, was in contrast focused on Lisbon, the centre of royal authority, and on the local merchant community, beholden to the Crown but essentially emancipated from feudal control.

In the fifteenth century, moreover, the external threat to Portugal was no longer over land. Spain was in such internal disarray that the frontier with her caused little concern to the Portuguese. The main external enemies were in fact the Moors across the sea. Thus, even external security considerations oriented the Portuguese state seaward.

The consequences of all this included not only Portugal's lead in discovering the sea-route to the East but the success of her caravels and galleons in wresting control of the Asian seas. The capture of Hormuz (1507), Goa (1510) and Malacca (1511) by Albuquerque gave Portugal monopoly control of the immensely lucrative spice trade[20] and set the stage for over four centuries of European domination of Asia. Not that Portugal had the manpower to participate actively in this trade. She left it largely in Asian hands. But from their citadel in Goa, the Portuguese licensed and policed foreign traders and extorted protection money. Of course, the origin of their domination lay in a mastery of the sea based on superiority in nautical technology and naval armament, which in turn reflected the comparative geopolitics of Asia and West Europe in an earlier era.

A possible counter-argument

Our story assigns a major role to state support of discovery and innovation in the early phases of open-ocean navigation and exploration. The Portuguese and Spanish states did provide such support. Nor were the English and Dutch states indifferent to maritime considerations: both the British crown and the States General of the Netherlands – as well as Philip II of Spain and Louis XIV of France – offered prizes for the best method of determining longitude at sea, and the British government enacted the Navigation Acts to achieve commercial supremacy and went to war repeatedly to enforce them. However, the British and Dutch states participated far less in maritime trade than the Portuguese or Spanish. Yet it was Holland and, especially, Britain that won the race for mastery of the seas. Claudia Rei[21] has in fact suggested that the long-run success of the British and the Dutch was due precisely to the lower involvement of the state than in Portugal or Spain. How does this square with our emphasis on state support?

There is, in fact, no contradiction. State support is indispensable only in the early phases of exploration and discovery, when the pioneers must run the risk of a leap in the dark largely for the generation of common knowledge, from the benefits of which none could be excluded. Portugal and Spain were the pioneers. The knowledge they created was freely available to latecomers like the English, the Dutch and the French despite the best efforts of the Iberian states to check its dissemination. On the other hand, the well-known costs and inefficiencies of government participation dogged the efforts of Spain and Portugal at every step; once the flow of new information tapered off and subsequent technical progress was reduced largely to learning by doing, they became millstones around the necks of the Iberian enterprises.

Why did the North Atlantic powers alone tap this newly created pool of common knowledge? Why not, for example, the Asian states? To some extent, indeed, Asia did try to assimilate Atlantic technology. Qing China commandeered Jesuit missionaries for the manufacture of artillery.[22] Late seventeenth- and eighteenth-century Indian states extensively hired European gunsmiths and mercenaries for their knowledge of gunpowder technology – so extensively, indeed, that the word for 'artilleryman' in many Indian languages is 'hollandaise'. But these events were small in scale, never substantial enough to induce the modernization of Indian or Chinese metallurgy. They were also limited in scope and never extended into the realm of maritime technology. What could be the possible explanation? It lay, of course, in the continental preoccupations of the Asian states. China's obsession with her Northern border was reinforced by continuing pressure from the nomads well into the seventeenth century: in fact, Ming rule was destroyed and replaced in 1644 by Northern invaders. In India, the North was defended by the Mughals until the end of the seventeenth century, but as soon as they weakened, the invaders flocked in. There was the devastating invasion of Nadir Shah in 1738. As late as 1761, on the eve of England's Industrial Revolution, when the British were already firmly entrenched in Bengal and Madras, the major event of Northern and Central India was the Third Battle of Panipat, at which the Northern invader, Ahmad Shah Abdali, defeated the Maratha Confederacy and ended their hopes of being the successor state to the Mughal empire. Even at this late date, no major Indian state could have shifted its focus from the land to the sea.

The geographic dimension of this factor is underlined by the fact that it did not affect the far South of the subcontinent. Buffered from the Northern invader by distance and many intervening kingdoms, the deep South was more aware of the threat posed by Europeans from the sea and keener to acquire their military technology and methods. In July 1741, Martand Verma, ruler of the tiny principality of Travancore, exploited the turbulent weather of the South West monsoon to blockade a Dutch expeditionary force in the coastal fort of Colachel, close to the Southernmost tip of India. The Dutch then ruled Sri Lanka and dominated significant parts of the Malabar coast. However, they were starved into surrendering at Colachel. The captured Dutch officers were inducted by Martand Verma into his army, where they were commissioned to equip Travancore forces with Western

38 Ocean navigation and the grand reversal

weapons and train them in Western military tactics. This they did to such effect that Travancore not only subjugated its immediate neighbours but also eventually induced the Dutch to abandon their pretensions to Malabar and withdraw to their Sri Lankan stronghold.[23]

Less successful but historically more important was Tipu Sultan, ruler some half a century later of the deep Southern kingdom of Mysore, who represented the greatest military threat faced by the British in eighteenth-century India. Tipu hired Dutch mercenaries to improve and man his artillery, which became a far more potent weapon than his own imaginative but rather ineffective device of rocket-borne missiles.

However, except for the far South, the Northern obsession continued to dominate the strategic thinking and policy of most Indian states in the early decades of European penetration into the Indian landmass. It affected not merely the geographic orientation of policy but the nature of the preferred military technology itself. As Hoffman[24] argues, both in China and India, the slow-firing and slower-moving artillery of contemporary gunpowder technology would have been ineffective against the swift cavalry of the Northern invaders. Indeed, the one major Indian indigenous (as distinct from foreign mercenary) artillery-based force – the 10,000-strong unit of Ibrahim Gardi – was annihilated at the Battle of Panipat by the Afghan cavalry. The Indian example is instructive for yet another, and closely related, reason. The focus on defence of the North during Mughal imperial domination had created certain institutions that catered primarily to the requirements of the cavalry – systems of honours and payments based on the grant of hereditary revenue rights to cavalier families. In the eighteenth century, the empire dissolved into a host of warring principalities rather like the European states system in its possibilities of competitive stimulation of military innovation. However, the vested interests of the local cavalier nobility precluded their dispossession by an alternative revenue system: states, therefore, were hard put for funds to finance an army based primarily on artillery and musket-bearing infantry.[25] Thus, it was not merely that the threat from Inner Asia persisted far longer in the Asian empires than in Europe; the inertia of institutions developed in response to these pressures hindered adjustment to a threat from a different quarter.

Alternative explanations

How does our story of the rise of the West compare with *four* other popular accounts of the same phenomenon?

Geoffrey Parker[26] has argued that the really significant point of divergence between the trajectories of the West and the rest was the Military Revolution, the transformation in European military technology and strategy in the early sixteenth century that guaranteed a growing superiority in military capacity. Certainly, such military superiority was an undeniable and overwhelming fact, initially limited in Asia to maritime conflicts but extending by the eighteenth century to land warfare as well. Just as undeniable was the role of this military hegemony in creating and perpetuating the political and economic subjugation of Asia. However, the crucial question concerns the origin of the divergence in military technology. This is a black box for Parker – and this is what our paper focuses on. In particular, we argue that this divergence was spearheaded by European innovations in naval artillery and architecture which were induced by open-ocean navigation and discovery and the resulting struggle for control of the new sea-routes. The crucial innovation in land warfare, efficient field-artillery, came almost 150 years later, possibly as a by-product of the demands that naval ordnance made on European metallurgy.

Jared Diamond[27] compares China with Western Europe and argues that China lagged behind as a consequence of the Ming withdrawal from the sea, which left the European navies in undisputed control of Asian waters. He claims that this basic policy error was never corrected because of the monolithic unitary character of imperial China. Such errors, he claims, could never persist in Europe because ruthless competition among a host of different states would eliminate those that make major errors. In turn, the differing geographies of China and Europe account for their differences in political structure – the continental imperial system of China as against the nation states of Europe with their maritime orientation, their many natural boundaries and small core areas. We agree with Diamond on the critical nature of the Ming withdrawal and the effects of geography on the political systems of Europe and Asia. However, it is an oversimplification to regard the Ming withdrawal as the unrectified mistake of a despotic regime or even as the simple triumph of the mandarin faction at court over the eunuch faction: it was, in our view, a reflection of the natural landward orientation of China and its traditional preoccupation with the Northern border, and it is this orientation that we have sought to explain.

Kenneth Pomeranz[28] (2000) has not only dated the divergence as late as the nineteenth century. He has also attributed it to two factors: (1) European, especially British, coal which provided the main energy inputs of the Industrial Revolution and (2) the agricultural and mineral resources of the New World which Europe could access readily and which enabled her to avert the Ricardian crisis of the early nineteenth century. While we do not go into the chronology of the divergence, we have a different account of its roots. Pomeranz ignores the abundance of coal in China: he believes that North China's rich coalfields could not stimulate Chinese industrialization because the Sung had been driven South of the Yangtse by the Jurchen invaders far out of reach of Northern coal. This could well be why a Sung industrialization was aborted despite all its technical innovations. However, the Ming Revolution of 1368 brought North China and its coal back into the Han orbit – so lack of coal is a less convincing explanation of the failure of China to take off even in the nineteenth century. And Europe's access to the Americas was a consequence of European exploration and trade, a phenomenon that needs to be explained rather than an exogenous circumstance: if China had explored the seas as vigorously, she could perhaps have discovered and accessed the natural resources of Australia and New Zealand (as she is doing now) at an earlier date.

40 Ocean navigation and the grand reversal

Finally, David Landes[29] attributes the success of Western Europe to a pre-existing spirit of scientific enquiry and openness to new ideas that sustained European technological dynamism well before the era of ocean navigation. He argues that in imperial Asia, such intellectual adventurousness was crushed by the dead weight of bureaucracy and imperial authority, while in Europe, competition between many small states facilitated dissent and intellectual innovation. In the ultimate analysis, therefore, he regards the differences in political structures between Asia and Europe as crucial but does not offer any explanation for them. We do.

All these accounts therefore leave unresolved major questions that we attempt to answer.

The growth effects of the West's domination of Asia

To complete our story, we need to touch, howsoever briefly, on the economic consequences for Asia of Western military and political dominance. How did this dominance translate into a rapidly widening economic gap between Europe and Asia?

The experience of countries that were formally colonized (such as India, Burma, Malaya, Indochina, Indonesia etc.) is best represented by the example of India. As with most issues in economic history, India's colonial experience is clouded by controversy about its facts as well as their interpretation. However, interpretations that veer to either extreme probably fly in the face of logic. Britain no doubt exploited her dominance over India for her own benefit, but the intensity of her exploitation was probably tempered by a reluctance to kill the goose that laid the golden eggs. Over the two centuries of her imperial rule, Britain graduated from the status of a 'roving bandit' to that of a 'stationary bandit', to use the language of Mancur Olson.[30] It all began in the mid-eighteenth century with rapacious plunder by East India Company officials inspired by the example of the first two governors, Robert Clive and Warren Hastings, and their assorted underlings, plunder that financed the rise of a whole new elite in Britain, the much-derided but unarguably super-rich 'nabobs'. It also probably induced the Bengal famine of 1770 that killed one-third of Bengal's population[31] and forced the abandonment of large tracts of the most fertile land in the country and the consequent erosion of taxable capacity and collapse in the share value of the East India Company. Second thoughts were inevitable after such a catastrophe. It dawned on the Company and the British government that they were in India for the long haul and that it was unnecessary and possibly counterproductive to get rich quick. A less extortionate and better-regulated regime evolved which concentrated on protecting the Company's and Britain's priorities. In 1793, the governor general, Lord Cornwallis, initiated the Permanent Settlement.[32] Eastern India was parcelled out to landlords (*zamindars*) who collected taxes on behalf of the Company, remitted 10/11ths of their collections to it and retained only 1/11th. These shares were rigidly fixed in perpetuity, supposedly as an incentive to the landlord to invest in his property. However, the landlord's share in the fruits of his investment was infinitesimal. Moreover, the smallness of this share meant that the landlord could not survive a bad harvest without defaulting, and any default meant that his land would be auctioned off. Landlords under the Permanent Settlement were too insecure to invest – and strongly motivated to maximize their extraction from the peasantry.

A main feature of this regime was the replacement of the entire Mughal aristocracy by a new, entirely British elite comprising the bureaucracy, military officialdom and private businessmen and technical experts. The first two elements of this elite enjoyed fabulous salaries, perquisites and pensions at the Indian taxpayer's expense. The salaries and profits of the private members of the British elite were protected by the British monopoly of the Indian product and job markets at the expense of the Indian consumer and producer. Bureaucratic salaries were equally prodigal. In 1901, the secretary of state for India, a Whitehall official who never needed to set foot in the country he administered, was paid out of Indian taxes a salary equal to the average income of 90,000 Indians.[33] For Britain, this meant handsome income and employment opportunities for a significant fraction of the British aristocracy, followed by luxurious retirement on pensions paid by the Indian taxpayer. After the take-over of India by the crown from the East India Company in 1858, it meant that British shareholders would be extravagantly compensated at Indian expense. And railway-building in India meant guaranteed bonds for British investors and generous dividends out of India's revenue. For India, it has been argued that there was a substantial reduction in the size of the elite and therefore in the tax burden it imposed on the rest of the economy. Even if this were true, the fact remains that the Mughal aristocracy spent its income in India, creating a large market for luxury manufactures in textiles, leather goods, furniture, carpets, ceramics, metalware, weapons and so on and resulting in an induced demand for activities like dyeing and brass and steel metallurgy. All this was lost because the British remitted their incomes to, or received them (as with pensions) in, Britain or spent them on imports from there. The multiplier effects of the new distribution of income were entirely positive for Britain and entirely negative for India. The craftsmen it displaced constituted a living burden on Indian agriculture that nullified the fiscal relief, if any, afforded by the new regime. In 1901, Digby estimated the net outflow from India to Britain over the previous century at 4.2 billion pounds.[34] Angus Maddison, with the benefit of a century of additional research, concludes that 'There can be no denial that there was a substantial outflow which lasted for 190 years'.[35]

A second feature of the regime was the creation of a large British Indian army. The entire officer corps of this army was British, but it was wholly paid, fed, armed and transported out of the Indian revenue. The army was deployed not only for completing the British conquest of India or quelling Indian rebellions but also for every foreign imperial venture that Britain chose, or was compelled, to embark on. This included the two world wars, in which India was not only required to supply military muscle to the British cause but also to lend vast sums to shore up British finances. The requirements of the army injected an element of 'military fiscalism' into the Indian revenue system and made it more rigid than would have been otherwise necessary.

42 *Ocean navigation and the grand reversal*

On the purely economic front, there was a conflict between the commercial objectives of Britain and especially those of the Company and her industrial interests. For most of its effective life, the East India Company's major exports were cotton textiles. These competed with British woollens and silks as well as with what was, in the eighteenth century, a still-nascent British cotton textile industry. The eighteenth-century compromise was to reserve the British market for British industry through outright bans on the import and possession of Indian cottons (the Calico Acts of 1700 and 1720) while permitting the Company to export calicoes freely to the rest of the world. However, once the Company acquired political power over Eastern India through its victories at Plassey (1757) and Buxar (1764), it began using this power to monopolize the textile trade. It sought to coerce weavers into diverting their business from Indian merchants to the Company, thus disrupting the traditional commercial network on which the expansion of the textile trade throughout the Indian market and abroad has been based. This culminated in the ban in 1770 of the *dadni* system of advances by Indian merchants to artisans for their working capital and subsistence requirements in exchange for a promise of delivery on a specific date of a given quality and quantity of product. The Company's monopsony undermined the bargaining power of the weavers and their real wage: the artisan's grain wage, estimated by Prasannan Parthasarathi[36] to exceed that of contemporary British weavers in 1750, declined rapidly thereafter. Indian merchant capital in the textile industry, too, was substantially destroyed. The fiscal requirements of the Company's administration and military also meant significant internal duties on the major traded good of the country. Imports from Britain and the products of British factories in India were exempt from these tolls. In 1825, these tolls were mostly abolished; the 70–80% tariffs on calico imports into Britain that had replaced the earlier absolute bans were also sharply reduced. However, the playing field was still far from level. British manufacturers paid only a 2% tariff for entry into India, but in 1831, a petition for withdrawal of a 10% tariff on Indian goods at British ports was rejected by Parliament. In 1835, Lord Ellenborough, president of the Board of Trade and soon-to-be governor general, told the Select Committee of the House of Commons that Indian textiles in their own country paid duties on raw material, yarn and dyeing processes that added up to 17% of their value. It is possible, of course, that, even without these handicaps, indigenous handloom products would have been driven out of the market by the machine-made textiles of Lancashire. Certainly, machine-made yarn made handspun technologically obsolete, and from the 1830s, handlooms lost their export market and a major share of the domestic market to Lancashire, whatever the reasons. However, the handloom industry survived and continued to supply the domestic market with products that were non-competitive with machine-made cloth. Could the Indian cotton textile industry as a whole conceivably have held its own, at least in the domestic and Asian markets in the absence of discriminatory Imperial policy? Probably not unless it was mechanized – which implied substantial access to capital and technology. In Bengal, indigenous capital in cotton textiles had been effectively exterminated by 1825 when British machine-made cloth first invaded these markets – which perhaps explains why the first Indian textile mills were set up not there but in Bombay in the 1850s. As for technology, British efforts to hinder its international diffusion by banning export of textile machinery and migration of textile workers were foiled by the clandestine flight of Samuel Slater to the United States. However, while the Indian cotton mills survived and even indeed invaded the Chinese market, in the absence of infant industry protection – such as the British textile industry enjoyed all the way up until 1825 – its recapture of the domestic market was painfully slow. It was well into the twentieth century that it received protection under the system of Imperial Preference – against Japan but certainly never against Britain. The palmy days of 1700–1750, when India enjoyed a 25% share in world textile exports and a 27% share in global manufacturing[37] were by then a distant memory.

A second important industry in the late seventeenth and early eighteenth century was ship-building. Indian ships built all along the coast, but especially in Bengal, were prized as commercial vehicles the world over, partly because of the exceptional durability of the teak of which they were constructed and partly because of the skill and experience of Indian shipwrights in working with this timber. The demand for them mounted with the rapid disappearance of oak forests in Britain and elsewhere in Europe as shipping fleets increased in size during the Commercial Revolution. The quality and cheapness of ships built in India meant low freight rates and stimulated the Indian shipping industry, both in coastal and international trade. But once Britain became politically dominant, she extended the Navigation Acts to Indian waters. All trade from and to ports controlled by Britain had now to be carried in British vessels. Duties were imposed on Indian – but not on British – ships even for coastal trade. Indian ships enjoyed a temporary reprieve during the Napoleonic Wars, when British fleets were severely depleted and Britain was forced to designate Indian ships and crew as 'British' for the purposes of the Navigation Act, but this interlude ended with Britain's victory.[38] The premature demise of capital and skill in the Indian shipping and ship-building industries was ensured well before the advent of the metal steam-ship.

A third industry of interest was the steel industry. India had an international reputation as the producer of fine crucible steel – the material of the famous Damascus sword – the composition of which has only recently been discovered after many centuries of intensive research by scientists as eminent as Michael Faraday.[39] The demand for this product of highly skilled small-scale manufacturers arose essentially from the weapons industry. After 1857, private possession of weapons by Indians was outlawed, as indeed were mining and extraction of metals (like lead and, of course, Damascus steel[40] [1884]) with any military possibilities whatsoever – and this industry died a sudden death. Steel-making, in its modern incarnation, was of course resurrected early in the twentieth century by the Tatas and given a fresh lease on life, not by colonial policy but by the world wars.

The British government sought, both before and after its direct assumption of power in 1858, quite explicitly to transform India into a captive market for British manufactures and a source of material for its commerce and industry. Indian agriculture was diverted from foodgrains to opium for the China trade, indigo

44 Ocean navigation and the grand reversal

and cotton for British textile production, jute for packaging and tea for the world market. Large-scale commercialization of the economy imposed burdens on the transport network, as did the military requirements of empire. This prompted the construction of an extensive railway system in the second half of the nineteenth century. The railways served Britain's strategic and commercial needs. They were also a highly profitable outlet for British capital (with returns guaranteed by the Indian government at rates far above international levels) that, in the first twenty years of railway development, absorbed 20% of all British portfolio investment. The capital cost of the Indian railways was hugely inflated: in the 1860s and 1870s, the cost per mile was nine times that of the United States contemporaneously, and, even after the British government's take-over of construction in the 1880s, it amounted to twice the cost per mile of railway building in Canada or Australia. Thanks to the subsidized freight rates that British traders enjoyed, the railways made little profit, but the British investor's guaranteed returns were dutifully sustained by the Indian taxpayer. Every piece of equipment used by the Indian railways was imported from Britain up to the First World War. All even minimally skilled jobs in the railways were reserved for the British or, later, the Anglo-Indians and paid for at wages far above Indian levels. The Indian railways represented a vehicle for a vast transfer of income from India to British investors, manufacturers, traders and workers. But they also had unintended consequences. They reduced procurement and distribution costs for domestic industry, improved labour mobility, extended the market and induced regional specialization. They generated economies of scale *à la* Adam Smith and led in the late nineteenth century to a slow economic growth which, while sluggish by most standards, yet contrasted sharply with the catastrophic decline of the previous 120 years. Parts of this process were the Bombay cotton mills and the revival of regionally specialized handicrafts and handloom products. Adding some momentum to the process was the development of large-scale irrigation for export agriculture, particularly of wheat and cotton from the Punjab, though the total investment in irrigation was only a ninth of the outlay on railways.

Perhaps the most corrosive effect of colonial subjugation was on the incentives of the subject population. With a very visible ceiling set by ethnic discrimination on the heights to which Indians could aspire to reach, there was little inducement for them to work, save, invest, acquire skills or take risks. Low economic and social mobility was a pervasive fact of life to which every Indian in British India had to adjust. Some succeeded in rising as far in the hierarchy as was permitted but had any further ambitions thwarted by the *raj*. Most preferred not even to try.

In sum, the colonial enterprise was designed for the benefit of Britain, largely at the expense of the colony, but it did produce some collateral benefits for India. These stemmed from railway building, the unification and pacification of the internal market and, to a lesser extent, from large-scale irrigation. It is highly improbable that, for India, the benefits of colonization outweighed the costs. One indicator of this is the frequency and intensity of famines. Indian agriculture has always been vulnerable to the caprices of the South West monsoon so that harvest failure and consequent famine have been recurring motifs in Indian history. However, there is general agreement that the heyday of the *raj*, the 'late eighteenth and nineteenth centuries were India's time of famine'.[41] The fifty years following the Crown's assumption of authority in India witnessed 24 major famines and affected long-term population growth despite the fact that this was also the era of railway building and should therefore have seen a reduced incidence of famines. Only in the twentieth century did famine become largely obsolete – though the British did not leave India without the parting gift of the essentially man-made Bengal famine of 1943, which killed four million people through starvation and the diseases that the resulting loss of immunity induced.

Recent scholarship (Broadberry and Gupta,[42] Allen)[43] suggests that the British inherited an already-impoverished India – if not from the Mughals, at least from the chaotic aftermath of the death of Aurangzeb (Clingingsmith and Williamson)[44] and that the *raj* can only be accused therefore of widening a preexisting divergence, not of engineering a reversal of fortune. The calculations of Prasannan Parthasarathi[45] showing that the real wages of weavers in Bengal and Karnataka around the time of Plassey matched, or perhaps exceeded, those of contemporary Englishmen cast some doubt on this point of view. However, there is general consensus on the opinion that the colonial regime did little or nothing to improve India's status in absolute terms while drastically undermining its relative position in the hierarchy of nations. In the sixty years before Independence, India's per capita GDP in 1990 international dollars had crawled from around $557 to $617 – a bare 10% increase. In the next six decades, it surged to $2975, a 482% multiplication that illuminates the economic benefits of self-rule and the calamitous consequences of colonial subjugation.[46]

Conclusion

Why did state-sponsored innovation in open-ocean navigation and naval warfare – the drivers of the course of modern economic growth and the determinants of the future spatial distribution of output – emerge in Atlantic Europe rather than in Asia or the rest of Europe? Our discussion previously has sought to address this problem in some detail. Here we focus narrowly on the key factors behind the location of this innovation drive.

First, the economic geography of the age of immobility separated sea-based trade into two geographically distinct circuits. This, combined with very high transport costs, made trade insignificant and ensured that the richest trade was over land. Advantages in land transport via horse breeding were a major force behind the economic and military might of the nomads of the Central Asian steppes. Thus, Asia in the Middle Ages was oriented towards land. The steppe nomads were secure in their ever-expanding economic and military power, while the great empires of the fertile alluvial river valleys of Asia created large enough agricultural surpluses to support and defend themselves and overshadow their coastal areas. These Asian empires, therefore, had no incentive to be interested in the sea and indeed sought to reduce the ability of coastal towns to emerge as independent political powers. The nomads were not interested in sea power either, as the main sources of their

46 Ocean navigation and the grand reversal

power – the mobility conferred by the horse and the fact that land-based high-value trade passed through their dominion – were unconnected with the ocean. Similarly, Mediterranean Europe was content with its dominion over the Mediterranean trade and had no particularly strong incentive to innovate further.

Western (Atlantic) Europe, in contrast, had strong incentives to develop the technology associated with open-ocean navigation and naval warfare. Geographical factors – the lack of large alluvial river valleys, as well as the fact that patches of fertile soil were separated by mountains, marshes and forests – were partly responsible for this. The natural barriers separating patches of fertile soil led to the emergence of a number of relatively small states, all in fierce competition with each other. Competition was thus a driver of innovation. Moreover, the absence of vast agricultural surpluses from the hinterland meant that ports were free to develop; the coast was not overshadowed by powerful land-based interests. There was no parallel to the continental empires of Asia. The thick forests West of the Hungarian steppe also sheltered Western Europe in relative security so that it was safe from the constant depredations of the steppe invaders. All these factors created an environment in which state-subsidized experimentation in navigation and naval warfare could flourish and lead to successful innovation. The Mediterranean countries did not need this, but the Atlantic countries, confronting the technological challenge of navigation in the open ocean, did. Among the Atlantic countries, moreover, the Iberian states were uniquely fitted for a pioneering role because they could tap existing seafaring skills and knowledge already developed in the Mediterranean.

The interplay between geography and the economics of transport in the era preceding that of open-ocean navigation thus created an economic and geopolitical distribution of power that resulted in spatial differences in the incentives of governments to sponsor innovation in open-ocean technologies. This is a rather different effect from the *direct* effect of (unchanging) geography on economic growth via proximity to the coast, proximity to rivers and climate that many other scholars have expertly explored.

Notes

1 A substantial part of this chapter, from the section headed 'The economic geography of medieval transport' to that headed 'Alternative explanations', is closely based on a joint paper by my daughter Brishti and me, published in *Revista di Storia Economica* in 2014. We are very grateful to the editors of the journal for permitting us to include this in the present volume.
2 For details on Atlantic winds, see Parry, *Discovery of the Sea*, 1981.
3 O. Lattimore, *The Inner Asian Frontiers of China*, 1940.
4 J. Saunders, *History of the Mongol Conquests*, 1971.
5 C. Stephenson, *Medieval Feudalism*, 1942.
6 P. Crone, *Slaves on Horses*, 1980.
7 J. Saunders, *History of the Mongol Conquests*, 1971.
8 J. Saunders, *History of the Mongol Conquests*, 1971.
9 E. L. Jones, *The European Miracle*, 1981.
10 C. Cipolla, *Guns, Sails and Empires*, 1965.

11 In enclosed waters, things were different, at least for a few centuries – as illustrated by the failure of the English and the French to secure a foothold in the Red Sea.

12 C. Cipolla, *Guns, Sails and Empires*, 1965.

13 A. J. Qaiar, Ship-Building in the Mughal Empire in the Seventeenth Century, *Indian Economic and Social History Review*, 1968.

A. J. Hourani, *Arab Seafaring in the Indian Ocean*, 1995.

14 C. Cipolla, *Guns, Sails and Empires*, 1965.

15 R. Menard, Transport Costs and Long-Range Trade 1300–1800, in J. Tracy (ed.), *Political Economy of Merchant Empires, 1350–1750*, Cambridge: Cambridge University Press, 1991.

R. W. Unger (ed.), *Shipping and Economic Growth, 1350–1850*, 2011.

16 K. H. O'Rourke, J. G. Williamson, Did Vasco da Gama Matter for European Markets? *The Economic History Review*, 62, 2009, pp. 655–684.

17 Lattimore, O., *Inner Asian Frontiers of China*, 1940.

M. Rossabi, *China and Inner Asia from 1368 to the Present Day*, 1975.

18 J. Needham, *Science and Civilization in China*, 2008.

19 M. Huan, *Ying Yai Sheng Lan (Overall Survey of the Ocean's Shores)*, 1433, J. V. G. Mills (tr. and ed.), London: Cambridge University Press, 1970.

L. Levathes, *When China Ruled the Seas: The Treasure Fleet of the Dragon Throne*, 1997.

20 D. B. Freeman, *The Straits of Malacca, Gateway of Gauntlet*, 2003.

21 C. Rei, The Organization of Eastern Merchant Empires, *Explorations in Economic History*, 48, 2011, pp. 116–135.

22 J. Waley-Cohen, China and Western Technology in the Late Eighteenth Century, *The American Historical Review*, 98 (5), 1993, pp. 1525–1544.

23 F. P. Miller, A. F. Vandome, J. McBrewster, *The Battle of Colachel*, 2010.

S. Subramanyam, The South Travancore and Mysore, 'India', in *Encyclopaedia Britannica*.

W. G. Noble, Kerala, in *Encyclopaedia Britannica*.

24 P. T. Hoffman, Why Was It Europeans Who Conquered the World? *The Economic History Review*, 72, 2012, pp. 601–633.

25 S. Gordon, The Limited Adoption of European-Style Military Forces by Eighteenth Century Rulers in India, *The Indian Social and Economic History Review*, 35 (3), 1998.

26 G. Parker, *The Military Revolution*, 1988.

27 J. Diamond, *Guns, Germs and Steel: The Fates of Human Societies*, 1997.

28 K. H. Pomeranz, *The Great Divergence: China, Europe and the Modern World Economy*, 2000.

29 D. S. Landes, Why Europe and the West? Why Not China? *Journal of Economic Perspectives*, 20 (2), 2006.

30 M. Olson, *Power and Prosperity: Outgrowing Communist and Capitalist Dictatorships*, New York: Basic Books, 2000.

31 R. K. Ray, Indian Society and the Establishment of British Supremacy, 1765–1818, in P. J. Marshall (ed.), *The Oxford History of the British Empire. Volume II: The Eighteenth Century*, Oxford: Oxford University Press, 1998, pp. 508–529.

32 R. Guha, *A Rule of Property for Bengal: An Essay on the Idea of Permanent Settlement*, Durham: Duke University Press, 1996.

33 W. Digby, *'Prosperous' British India: A Revelation from Official Records*, London: T. Fisher Unwin, 1901.

34 W. Digby, *'Prosperous' British India: A Revelation from Official Records*, London: T. Fisher Unwin, 1901.

35 A. Maddison, *Class Structure and Economic Growth: India and Pakistan Since the Moghuls*, New York: Routledge, 2013.

36 P. Parthasarathi, Rethinking Wages and Competitiveness in the Eighteenth Century: Britain and South India, *Past and Present*, 158 (1), 1998, pp. 79–109.

37 A. Maddison, *Development Centre Studies The World Economy Historical Statistics*, OECD Publishing, 2003.

48 Ocean navigation and the grand reversal

38 Most of the information on Indian shipping and ship-building is from I. Ray, Ship-building in Bengal under Colonial Rule: A Case of 'DeIndustrialisation', *The Journal of Transport History*, 16 (1), 1995.

39 S. Srinivasan, S. Ranganathan, *India's Legendary Wootz Steel: An Advanced Material of the Ancient World*. Iron & Steel Heritage of India, 2004.

40 Sir R. F. Burton, *The Book of the Sword*, London: Chatto & Windus, 1884.

41 B. Currey, G. Hugo, *Famine as a Geographical Phenomenon*, Boston: GeoJournal library, 1984.

B. Murton, VI.4: Famine, in *The Cambridge World History of Food*, vol. 2, New York: Cambridge University Press.

42 S. Broadberry, B. Gupta, The Early Modern Great Divergence: Wages, Prices and Economic Development in Europe and Asia, 1500–1800, *Economic History Review*, 59 (1), 2006, pp. 2–31.

43 R. C. Allen, India in the Great Divergence, in T. J. Hatton, K. H. O'Rourke, A. M. Taylor, (eds.), *The New Comparative Economic History: Essays in Honor of Jeffery G. Williamson*, Cambridge, MA: MIT Press, 2007.

44 D. Clingingsmith, J. G. Williamson, Deindustrialization in Eighteenth and Nineteenth Century India, *Explorations in Economic History*, 45 (3), 2008, pp. 209–234.

45 P. Parthasarathi, Rethinking Wages and Competitiveness in the Eighteenth Century: Britain and South India, *Past and Present*, 158 (1), 1998, pp. 79–109.

P. Parthasarathi, Cotton Textiles in the Indian Subcontinent, 1200–1850, in P. Parthasarathi, G. Riello (eds.), *The Spinning World: A Global History of Cotton Textiles, 1200–1850*, Oxford and New York: Oxford University Press, 2011.

46 A. Maddison, *Statistics on World Population, GDP and Per Capita GDP, 1–2008 AD*, 2010.

4

A SHORT NOTE ON NEW WORLD REVERSALS

We have explored the impact of the West European innovations in maritime technology on Asia. Their impact on the New World of the Americas and Australasia began earlier and more dramatically and lasted at least as long, if not longer. There was, however, no immediate reversal of fortune. After the lightning military conquest of the Aztec and Inca empires through Spanish fire-power and cunning diplomacy, there remained no indigenous states to serve as yardsticks of wealth and power. The sophisticated pre-existing civilizations were totally destroyed. Indeed, beginning with Columbus in Hispaniola and continuing with his successors in Mesoamerica and the rest of Iberian America, there occurred throughout the sixteenth century an extermination of the indigenous population through disease, malnutrition and genocide estimated by some experts at 90% or more. In the virtual vacuum thus created, the Spanish and the Portuguese set up their own institutions and societies. The British, the French and the Dutch did likewise after destroying indigenous societies all over the Americas and the Caribbean. How did these new societies measure up in economic potential and performance?

Three spectacular bursts of natural resource-based economic growth occurred in America between the Spanish conquest and the mid-nineteenth century.

1 The silver boom from the mid-sixteenth to the mid-seventeenth century based on the newly discovered mines of Zacatecas in Mexico and, especially, of Potosi in Bolivia.
2 The seventeenth and eighteenth century sugar boom in the Caribbean islands and Brazil.
3 The cotton boom in the southern states of the United States in the early nineteenth century.

50 A short note on New World reversals

All three were triggered by and catered to explosions of demand in the outside world. The deluge of silver that poured out of Lima and Acapulco was attracted by Ming China's gradual transition to a silver currency and taxes paid in silver – whether it flowed directly into China via Manila or indirectly through Amsterdam and the European importers of Chinese silk, tea and porcelain. Brazil and the sugar islands of the Caribbean developed their plantations in response to the expanding world demand for sweetness. And the cotton of the Confederate states was the basic raw material of the Industrial Revolution, with its many-fold acceleration of spinning and weaving to supply mushrooming textile markets all over the world.

What were the supply conditions that facilitated these events? Geography was crucial, of course – the mineral endowment of Mexico and Bolivia, the climate and soil of the West Indies, of North East Brazil and the Southern United States. Just as indispensable, however, was labour. In the rarefied atmosphere of Potosi, at an altitude of 15,000 feet, far above the tree-line, a city of 160,000 – as populous as London or Paris at that time – had to be supplied, sustained and driven to life-sapping work in the silver mines. That this was possible at all was because of the abundance of labour in the Inca and Aztec territories and a long history of forced labour to which the population was accustomed. But as the silver era wore on, the population was decimated by disease, malnutrition and lethal conditions of work. African slaves had to be imported. In the plantation monocultures of the Caribbean and Brazil, slave labour was the norm from the outset. The Iberians had, in the fifteenth century, already established sugar plantations in Madeira, the Canaries, the Azores and Cape Verde, mid-Atlantic islands whose relative proximity to the West African slave markets facilitated the large-scale use of slave labour. With the discovery of America, the Madeira model was replicated wholesale in the Caribbean colonies and Brazil. Nor was this colonial institution confined to the Portuguese and Spanish territories like Brazil, Haiti (then Saint Domingue), Cuba and Puerto Rico. It was emulated enthusiastically by the British (Barbados, Jamaica etc.) and the French (Martinique, Grenada etc.). And, in the nineteenth century, this was the model that the United States adopted to power the astronomical growth of cotton cultivation throughout the Southern states, as it had done earlier for the tobacco plantations of Virginia and the sugar plantations of Louisiana. In 1793, Eli Whitney invented the mechanical cotton gin and, in the sixty years that followed, cotton plantations spread through the US South like wildfire. By 1860, cotton accounted for 60% of all US exports, and the GDP of the South was sky-rocketing.

In the global economy created by ocean navigation and the Discoveries, as long as international demand for the relevant commodity boomed, the supply regions flourished mightily. Their GDP soared, and they attracted immigrants and large-scale capital inflows. Their tropical climates and unhealthy disease environments did little to deter European settlers. The highly extractive institution of slavery that was central to their society did not retard their growth; indeed, it seemed to have stimulated it. In 1700, though the silver boom had petered out with the saturation of the Chinese demand for the metal, the per capita income of Mexico was still almost at par with that of the United States, while those of Barbados and Cuba were estimated as 50% and 67%, respectively, higher. These countries, along with Jamaica and Brazil, were, on a per capita basis (including slaves), then among the richest in the world. Even in 1800, round about the time of her revolution, Haiti was probably the world's richest economy. Lending further point to these comparisons is the fact that the US GDP itself was buoyed up by the output of the Southern slave plantations.[1]

It was from this point that the reversal of fortune in the Western Hemisphere commenced. As the Industrial Revolution in Western Europe accelerated, so did the settlement and development of the United States and Canada. Until the Civil War, King Cotton and the Southern states were leading participants in this process, but thereafter it was the expansion of the railway, of wheat cultivation in the prairie and of industry in the North East that powered it. By the turn of the century, Mexico, Brazil and the Caribbean countries were left far behind, and the Confederate states were trailing the rest of the United States. Over the next 95 years or so, these gaps only widened.

How does one explain this twist in the tale of Western Hemisphere growth? Engerman and Sokoloff (ES),[2] following in the footsteps of AJR,[3] attribute this to the superior economic efficiency of the institutions of the United States and Canada relative to those of Brazil and the Caribbean. The former developed inclusive institutions, arising out of and fostering an equitable distribution of income, wealth, economic and political power. Most importantly, this led to a demand for and public investment in education that created a skilled labour force, well equipped for the requirements of industry. It also created a large homogeneous middle-class market in which manufacturing could enjoy economies of scale. The latter set of countries, on the other hand, were characterized by a concentration of wealth and power in a planter or mining elite which had no interest in education or industrialization. In the age of industrialization, such institutional differences guaranteed the rapid growth of the former and the stagnation or decay of the latter.

But what led to these institutional differences? Obviously, and contrary to the AJR model for the world economy, it had nothing to do with the national origins of the colonists. The British and the French, who had created the institutions of the United States and Canada, had, when they migrated to and settled in Barbados, Jamaica and Martinique, established institutions hardly distinguishable from what the Spaniards developed in Haiti or Cuba or the Portuguese did in Brazil. Nor was it true that settlement patterns were dictated, as AJR believed, by the climate, disease conditions and mortality rates of the colonies. As long as there were fortunes to be made there, the Caribbean and the US South, despite their high mortality rates, attracted floods of settlers from Europe, Canada and the US North East.

In a classic but little-known paper in 1956, Robert Baldwin[4] explained the differences between regions like the US South, Brazil and the Caribbean on the one hand and the Midwest and North East of the United States on the other in terms of geography favouring crops with different production functions. The soils and climate of the North East and, especially, the Midwest encouraged cereal cultivation, annual crops that were ideal for family farms. The geography of the South

52 A short note on New World reversals

suited plantation crops better: tobacco and, especially, cotton. The differences in the optimal scales of production between family farms and plantations led to differences in the concentration of wealth and power and therefore in institutional structure between the two regions. On large plantations, slavery kept the cost of labour below what it would have been, but on family farms, it would have been ineffective and entirely inappropriate.

In the US South, however, as in the Caribbean and Brazil, the inequality of wealth and power survived the abolition of slavery and persisted well into the twentieth century. This could perhaps be accounted for by the AJR and ES notion of institutional inertia or of the long shadow cast by institutions of the past. A somewhat more mundane explanation runs, as Baldwin suggests, in terms of the production function of the dominant crop which shaped the factor endowment of the economy, would have done so if slavery never existed and continued to do so even after slavery disappeared. The factor requirement of the dominant activity was a large quantity of unskilled labour which was supplied earlier by slavery. Subsequently, in the West Indies and Guyana, African slaves were replaced by indentured Chinese and Indian immigrants imported under contracts that differed only in name from slavery. This was the system employed elsewhere in the world as well, wherever in fact geography and labour requirements were similar in the late nineteenth and early twentieth centuries, in the sugar plantations of Mauritius and Fiji, the rubber plantations of Malaya, the tea plantations of India and Sri Lanka, the railway construction projects of East and South Africa. In the US South, the legacy of slavery was a large surplus of unskilled black labour. This added to the unskilled white labour – the so-called 'white trash' imported by investors in plantations under indenture contracts that restricted its freedom to move. Post-bellum, this labour surplus was very slow to dissipate. Many generations passed before the uncertain if better-paid prospects of a totally different kind of work in a distant and alien environment could induce the emancipated but uneducated slave to leave the familiar if unpleasant security of the Southern plantation *en masse*. Meanwhile, the continued presence of this army of labour depressed wages, prolonged poverty and inequality and delayed industrialization in the South.

The differences in the tempo of industrialization of the two sets of regions in the New World were firmly rooted in the production functions of the activities that dominated the economies of each before industrialization: they were consequences of the interaction of technology with geography. This was the Baldwin thesis, rediscovered, confirmed and elaborated by ES.

Allen, Murphy and Schneider[5] (AMS) argue that the different development paths of Latin and North America reflect not geographical differences but differences in the wage levels of the countries from which the settlers in these colonies originated. As a rule, people migrate only if the wages they expect at their destination compensate for their current wages plus the cost of moving. From the mid-seventeenth century, when British migration into North America began, British real wages were at least twice the Spanish level; therefore, British settlers expected and received substantially higher incomes than contemporary Iberian migrants. The

Baldwin-Engerman-Sokoloff consequences followed – though the causes were quite different from what they had imagined.

The AMS story fits the comparative economic history of the United States on the one hand and Mexico and Peru on the other. The Caribbean islands and Brazil might be another matter. The sugar colonies all followed similar economic trajectories regardless of the country of origin of their settlers. In fact, AMS's Latin American wage data are from Mexico, Bogota and Potosi, not from the sugar colonies at all. And, unlike Baldwin, AMS do not provide a plausible account of the reversal of fortune *within the United States* between the Confederate states and the rest of the country.

Regardless of whether one prefers the AMS model or the Baldwin account, the primacy of one region or another in any period undoubtedly reflected the shifting conditions of demand in the international market created by transport innovations. The age of silver and Spain reflected the rise and fall of the demand for silver in Ming China in the sixteenth and early seventeenth centuries. The success of Brazil and the Caribbean economies was linked to Europe's growing addiction to sugar during the Commercial Revolution of the seventeenth and eighteenth centuries. The heyday of cotton and the US South was associated with the astronomical expansion of the cotton textile industry in the first sixty years of Britain's Industrial Revolution. These three successive phases of the New World's development were all linked to the growth of maritime trade. But the rise of the North East and the Midwest of the United States depended not only on sea trade but also on a revolution in inland transport: it gathered momentum as food scarcities mounted in Europe in the wake of the Industrial Revolution and as railways reached across the prairie towards the frontier and beyond.

It is necessary at this point to illuminate a crucial component of our argument. Why were silver, sugar and cotton so closely associated with forced labour and, indeed, with slavery? And why did cereal cultivation encourage the growth of family farms?

Free labour will not agree to do very unpleasant work unless paid very high wages – and even then it must be closely monitored to ensure that it does not shirk the most unpleasant tasks. With forced labour, the high wages can be replaced by what the economist euphemistically calls 'pain incentives' – the lash, or the fear of it. Psychologists agree that the lash can induce intense observable effort, but not care or skill. Therefore, employers tend to use forced labour in activities that are intensive in unpleasant effort whenever this option is available.[6] Silver mining and tropical sugar and cotton plantations in the age before mechanization all qualify. At Potosi, the lethal character of work in an airless mine at an altitude where oxygen is very scarce anyway is evident. On the sugarcane and cotton plantations, apart from the sheer unpleasantness of the work, there were other considerations that encouraged the use of slave labour.

Sugarcane needs to be processed as close as possible to the point and time of harvest. It loses more value through desiccation and evaporation the longer the time-lapse between harvest and crushing. It also loses much of its weight and bulk

54 A short note on New World reversals

during processing, so that transport costs are greatly reduced if this is done on the farm itself rather than at a distant mill – a factor that was all the more crucial in a period when land transport had yet to be revolutionized by the innovations of the railroad and the internal combustion engine. All this meant that sugarcane farms equipped with large processing machinery had a huge cost advantage over farms that were not. In order to use their equipment at full capacity, such farms had to be very large – far too large, in fact, to be family enterprises. They had to depend on hired wage labour or slaves and, since free labour always had the option of alternative wage employment (and, in the United States, of moving to free land on the frontier), slavery represented the simplest way of minimizing labour costs.

Economies of scale, though not quite as pronounced, also existed on cotton plantations, due to factors like the mechanical gin. This meant that family enterprises could rarely compete with larger farms. Also, since the most important component of work was harvesting, in which individual effort could be easily monitored (by simply measuring the volume of the crop brought in by each worker), supervisory costs were not too high in non-family units. As with sugar, a significant edge therefore existed for slave labour in cotton over free labour or family farms.

Not so, however, in care-intensive activities. These included artisanal manufactures characteristic of the early phases of industrialization. They also included seasonal or annual field-crops, particularly cereal cultivation. Output in these forms of agriculture is the joint product of many different operations (preparing the ground, sowing, irrigation, fertilization, weeding etc.), all separated by long gestation periods from the harvest, so that it is impossible to isolate the contribution of any individual to production. Output-based schemes of payment for labour do not work except in harvesting. And, since work is also prohibitively costly to monitor if scattered all over a large farm, input-based schemes don't work either. Inability to monitor labour rules out not just slavery but wage labour and capitalist agriculture as well. Only fixed-rent tenancy or peasant ownership with family farming make sense. This, of course, is why the wheat boom of the late nineteenth century was also a boom in family farming, creating a reasonably affluent middle class that wanted schools and constituted a homogeneous market for large-scale industrialization.

The reversal of fortune in the Americas in the nineteenth and twentieth centuries was the outcome of the shift in world demand from sugar and cotton to wheat as the Industrial Revolution came up against the limits imposed by land scarcity on European agriculture. This was what led to the penetration of the American prairie by the railway, its rapid settlement and the expansion of cultivation of a crop that had beneficial effects on industrial development.

Certainly the Caribbean islands, Brazil and the US South had, in the 300 years after Columbus, acquired institutions that inhibited *industrialization* – while the North East and the Midwest of the United States had not. In part, these institutions reflected the technology of the economic activity that dominated the former set of regions. However, it is crucial to appreciate that these institutions did not, over three centuries, inhibit *GDP growth*. They may, in fact, have facilitated it. ES believe that in 1800, Haiti was the world's richest economy in terms of per capita GDP (taking slaves into account). Three hundred years is a long time – longer, in fact, then the age that has passed since. And over this length of time, the slave-driven economies of Barbados, Jamaica and Haiti outperformed the freer societies further North – if GDP growth is the yardstick of performance.

Undoubtedly, it was not *inclusive growth*: it was, in fact, about as inequitable as it is possible for an economy to be. That, however, is a separate issue. What the post-Columbian history of the Caribbean sugar islands and Brazil demonstrates is that sustained long-term GDP growth is quite possible with institutions that violate every canon of equality and freedom. The conclusion – ES's as well as AJR's – that long-term GDP growth requires freedom and inclusiveness are emphatically falsified by their evidence. They could be modified to assert that *inclusive growth* is associated only with inclusive institutions. But that would be virtually a tautology.

Notes

1 S. L. Engerman, K. L. Sokoloff, Institutions, Factor Endowments and Paths of Development in the New World, *Journal of Economic Perspectives*, 14 (3), 2000, pp. 217–232.

  D. Eltis, The Total Product of Barbados, *Journal of Economic History*, 55, 1995, pp. 321–336.

  R. B. Sheridan, The Wealth of Jamaica in the Eighteenth Century, *Journal of Economic History*, 18 (2), 1965, pp. 292–311.
2 S. L. Engerman, K. L. Sokoloff, Institutions, Factor Endowments and Paths of Development in the New World, *Journal of Economic Perspectives*, 14 (3), 2000, pp. 217–232.
3 D. Acemoglu, S. Johnson, J. A. Robinson, The Colonial Origins of Comparative Development: An Empirical Investigation, *American Economic Review*, 91, 2001, pp. 1369–1401.
4 R. E. Baldwin, Patterns of Development in Newly Settled Regions. *Manchester School of Economic and Social Studies*, 24 (2), 1956, pp. 161–179.
5 R. C. Allen, T. E. Murphy, E. B. Schneider, The Colonial Origins of the Great Divergence, A Labour Market Approach, *Journal of Economic History*, 91, 2001, pp. 1369–1401.
6 S. Fenoaltea, Slavery and Supervision in Comparative Perspective: A Model, *Journal of Economic History*, 44 (3), 1984, pp. 635–668.

5

THE FIRST INDUSTRIAL NATION AND ITS MANY REVERSALS OF FORTUNE

Britain's reversals of fortune

While the technology of ocean navigation turned the political hierarchy of continents upside down, it also produced major reversals of fortune between countries even within the increasingly dominant Western world. As an example of this process, we follow the fortunes of Britain, the pioneer of the Industrial Revolution, the 'Ruler of the Waves' and the greatest imperial power of the world since the Mongol empire.

Fifteenth-century Britain was an island kingdom of little consequence on the North Western periphery of a continent on which she fought for a hundred years to gain a foothold and failed. Ocean navigation changed her view of the world. By the end of the sixteenth century, she was a major contender for control of the sea-lanes of the world, her pirates and traders effectively challenging the Iberians, the Dutch and the French. There was also a nascent industrialization and urbanization process developing around England's sea-ports, a process that some historians have labelled 'the First Industrial Revolution'.[1] During the seventeenth century, however, this process was aborted, and Britain plunged into civil war and political turmoil. Meanwhile, the Iberians faded away as the centre of European economic activity shifted North-Westward from the Mediterranean. Holland emerged as the world's leading commercial power. But by the end of Holland's 'Golden Century', Dutch economic leadership, too, was under threat. A politically rejuvenated Britain in the midst of an Agricultural Revolution was posing a fresh threat at sea, a threat that eventually undermined Holland's commercial supremacy and paved the way for Britain's commercial and imperial hegemony. Throughout the eighteenth century, the rise of Britain continued, culminating in the Industrial Revolution that made her not only the mistress of the seas and of an empire over which the sun never sets but also the workshop of the world. Yet this, too, passed. From the last quarter of the nineteenth century, the rise of continental rivals, of the United States, Germany and Russia, rapidly eroded Britain's industrial leadership, creating a new hierarchy of developed countries that dominated the twentieth-century world.

Why did Britain overtake first Spain and then Holland in the race to build a trading network and a colonial empire? Why, then, did it succumb eventually to the challenge of the United States, Germany and Russia?

We argue that Britain's success against her initial rivals was due to her unique geographical advantages in the age of ocean navigation, while her eventual eclipse by her continental competitors reflected the fact that from the end of the nineteenth century, the railway and the automobile ensured that the dominant technology of transport was oriented toward the land rather than the sea.

Britain and the technology of ocean navigation

The remote but appropriate starting point for our chronicle of the rise and fall of Britain is the early fourteenth century. The Medieval Warm Period, 300 years of glorious summers and bountiful harvests, when the Norsemen established colonies in Labrador and the Danes settled Greenland, is over. The glaciers are back in the Arctic and the Alps as Europe slides slowly into the Little Ice Age. England, where the years of plenty have nurtured a population of some 4.8 million, faces year after year of harvest failure and famine. As malnutrition undermines people's immunities, a new and terrible killer appears – the plague. Beginning with the Black Death of 1348 which, in a single year, exterminates one-third of the population of Europe, the plague strikes England again and again. By the end of the century, the English number little more than 2 million. And, as epidemics and harvest failures and famine due to climate change persist, the number remains near this rock bottom for 150 years.[2] At the dawn of the Elizabethan era, England was a scantily populated pastoral economy, which, apart from its subsistence agriculture, was primarily in the business of wool production and export, the material and, increasingly, the textile. Thanks to 200 years of depopulation, labour was scarce, wages and living standards were high and land was plentiful enough to support pastoralism and produce enough food for a small population – when the weather permitted. The government, however, was chronically impecunious: the small size of the economy and the ample opportunities for tax evasion through smuggling that a long indented coastline offered meant that it was a constant struggle for the crown to make ends meet. Successive Tudor monarchs had to resort to a variety of devices for finance – borrowing in the Antwerp market, dissolution of the monasteries and confiscation of their assets, the sale of charters of monopoly, and consecutive debasements of the coinage under Henry VIII and Edward VI that initiated the inflationary spiral that is often blamed on the influx of bullion from the New World.

But in the middle of the sixteenth century, all this was about to change. By then, the knowledge of the technology of ocean navigation and warfare that Spain and Portugal had built up had slowly percolated to the North Sea countries. English

58 The first industrial nation

and Dutch borrowing or plagiarizing of this information is well documented. A few samples:

- Sebastian Cabot, the Italian-English mariner who claimed to have discovered Newfoundland, spent 30 years as pilot major at the Seville navigational academy before returning to England in 1548 to train Englishmen in the art of navigation and pioneer England's maritime explorations.
- Sir Francis Drake, while circumnavigating the globe, relied heavily on translations of two famous Spanish manuals, both entitled *The Art of Navigation*, by Pedro de Medina (1545) and Martin Cortes (1551). Not willing to leave anything to chance, he also abducted the Portuguese pilot Nuna de Silva for the passage to Brazil and down the East coast of America and, for the Pacific crossing, stole the charts and sailing directions of two Spanish pilots bound for Manila.[3]
- Edward Wright, in his classic *Certain Errors in Navigation* (1610), plagiarized large sections of Rodrigo Zamorano's *Compendium of the Art of Navigation*, published in Seville thirty years earlier.[4]

England was uniquely fitted by geography to exploit the technology she had thus acquired. An island just off the Atlantic coast of Europe, controlling access from the ocean to the North Sea, the Baltic, the Rhine and the Northern shores of France, was bound to become a principal node of the world transport network and a major cross-roads of trade. With her island immunity from invasion, she could, unlike her rivals, focus almost exclusively on the sea and on maritime warfare. At the same time, she was in a position to intercept the booming Atlantic trade of North West and Central Europe.

The late Elizabethan era saw the beginnings of England's oceanic ventures. These were initially piratical, but with exploratory and commercial components added when opportunity offered. The plunder of Spanish treasure ships laden with silver from the Potosi mines, the interception of Spain's trade in woollen cloth with Antwerp, the capture of Portuguese carracks returning from Indian Ocean voyages via the Azores or much further away in the Straits of Malacca – these were the primary objectives of English seamen. John Hawkins also pioneered what was to become a staple of British commerce, the triangular trade whereby Englishmen captured or bought slaves in West Africa for sale in the Caribbean in exchange for silver, sugar or other New World products for British consumption or reexport to Europe.

However, Britain's new maritime aggressiveness also benefited her wool producers and manufacturers and the merchants who sold the products in the Baltic and the Netherlands *entrepots*. It also meant increased demand for ships and weapons. Wood was the essential raw material for ships and iron for weapons. The extraction of iron – and, indeed, of other metals, too – from the ore required charcoal-smelting, which added to the demand for wood. Each enterprise of trade or piracy was an investment: it required financing and perhaps insurance. The new sea routes therefore generated demand near the ports for seamen as well as for ship-building, metallurgy, iron-mining, mercantile, banking and insurance services and, within easy distance, for wool production and manufacture. They created local concentrations of income and population, which in turn attracted market-oriented industries and increased demand for food, fuel and housing. Fuel and housing required even more wood – and, since wood is expensive to transport, these demands had to be met from local sources near the nuclei of income and population. All the while, local supply was contracting due to deforestation, not just for the sake of the timber but also to clear land for arable or pasture.

The crisis of the seventeenth century and its resolution

Britain was fabulously well endowed with coal within easy access of water transport along rivers or the coast. Throughout the late sixteenth century, the demand for wood was tempered by its gradual replacement as domestic or industrial fuel by coal. In domestic heating; in the production of sea-salt; in pottery; in the manufacture of bricks and glass, alum, soap and saltpetre; even in much non-ferrous metallurgy, coal could be substituted for wood with relatively little technical difficulty. Even in construction, wood could be replaced to some degree by bricks baked in coal-fired kilns. But wood remained irreplaceable in ship-building and iron-smelting – and both these were crucial components of the new maritime economy. From the 1620s, a timber crisis was in the offing. Throughout the seventeenth century, as the scarcity of wood and domestic iron mounted, Britain became increasingly dependent on the Baltic for these vital imports.

Meanwhile, however, a deeper crisis had overtaken the country. England's population, decimated by the Black Death and its century-long aftermath, had bottomed out in the mid-fifteenth century. Since 1450, it had been increasing steadily. Given the initial abundance of land, food supply was elastic to begin with, and early population growth was easily absorbed. But growth accelerated from the middle of the sixteenth century: population rose by 45% between 1541 and 1600 and nearly 30% between 1600 and 1650. Population was not just redistributing itself towards ports and industry. It was exploding (by pre-industrial standards) in absolute numbers as well. Diminishing labour productivity returned to agriculture, and the real wage dropped disastrously in the early seventeenth century. However, intermittent population growth continued for a while.

To understand the persistence of population growth – albeit slowing population growth – at a time of plummeting living standards, we need to look at its determinants. First, wages were still above subsistence so that, in normal years, without a disastrous sequence of epidemics and famines, mortality would be affected, but not in a major way. Fertility would be the main channel through which real wages could impinge on demographics. In a pre-industrial society, fertility behaviour was largely a matter of two factors: the age of first marriage of women and the proportion of women who never marry. Economic forces – employment opportunities and real wages – influence these variables since people decide whether and when to marry on the basis of their estimate of the possibility of supporting an independent family after marriage. However, these factors operate only with long lags. Marriage

60 The first industrial nation

is a long-term investment, so the decision to marry is based not on short-term fluctuations in income prospects but on well-established and generally perceived long-run trends in living standards and job opportunities. Even after marriage, there is a significant and elastic interval before children are born. The drop in real wages checked population growth only after many years – perhaps even a generation – and its impact was diluted by the fact that, thanks to the new sea routes, employment in London and around other ports and in the manufacture of woollen textiles tapered off only slowly even when food prices were shooting up and the real wage in agriculture plunged. By the mid-seventeenth century, however, population growth had levelled off and was sometimes being reversed.

The first half of the seventeenth century saw the overlap of a timber crisis that tended to arrest industrial growth and a food crisis that sharply reduced living standards. It nurtured discontent on a massive scale with any institution that appeared to constrain industrial or agricultural growth. The most obvious of these were the Crown's demands for taxes from Parliament. Others included the forest rights of the king and the greater nobles, which restricted the supply of wood for industry and of land for agriculture; the authority of the monarch to sell charters of monopoly which restricted entry into the monopolized fields of activity and the Court of the Star Chamber, which, apart from being the king's instrument for arbitrary and oppressive legal decision-making, was also the main judicial barrier to enclosure of the commons that many (especially the landed gentry in Parliament) believed was the solution to the agricultural problem. The expanding opportunities for trade enriched a handful of monopolists while stirring the envy of many. They created a revolution of rising aspirations among large groups of merchants and squires, aspirations that were thwarted by the restrictive old order.

Despite the divine right to rule claimed by the Stuarts, conflicting interests of such intensity at a time of such crisis led inevitably to revolution. They precipitated a bloody civil war ending in the arrest and decapitation of the ruling monarch, the installation first of Parliamentary rule and then of the Protectorate of Oliver Cromwell under the Commonwealth, the Restoration of the Stuarts and their eventual eviction in the Glorious Revolution of 1688. Sixty years of chaos ended in the replacement of a rigid absolutist regime by a constitutional monarchy, largely responsible to Parliament and therefore responsive at least to the economic interests of the gentry – the new Whig oligarchy of capitalist farmers and their mercantile allies who dominated the Commons. By the end of the seventeenth century, enclosures had acquired a new momentum, so that restrictions on land use disappeared. Serfdom had long been replaced by wage labour, eliminating feudal restrictions on labour mobility. Joint stock companies, the principle of limited liability and the stock market had evolved, reducing the risks of capital investment. The Bank of England had been established, making lending a safer proposition. The Statute of Monopolies (1624) so circumscribed the king's power to sell charters of monopoly as to become essentially a Patent Act for the protection of innovations from imitation. The foundations of a free market had been laid.

The failure of Spain

Not entirely, though. England's eventual triumph over her principal North Atlantic rival was in part based on a major trade restriction transformed into a weapon of war in order to exploit her geopolitical advantages. This is part of the tale of the struggle for maritime supremacy between the English and the Dutch which erupted in the mid-seventeenth century with Spain's eventual recognition of the independence of the United Provinces. By then, however, Spain, which was the pioneer and initial beneficiary of the Age of Discovery, was no longer a serious contender for European supremacy, and we should perhaps pause to examine the reasons for Spain's decline before embarking on the story of the Anglo-Dutch struggle.

In the mid-sixteenth century, Spain appeared to be the mightiest power in Europe. The discoveries and the brutal conquest of the Aztec and Inca empires had left her in control not only of the Atlantic islands and the Caribbean but also of Central America, Andean South America and the Philippines. The ascent of the Habsburgs to the Spanish throne had added to Spain's possessions most of Central Europe and the Low Countries. As trans-Atlantic trade and settlement developed and were funnelled through Seville, manufacturing, shipping and urbanization boomed and population increased, generating an increased demand for food. Given the abundance of idle land in Spain in the early 1500s, agriculture could expand to cater to this demand without initially running into diminishing returns. There was also an inflow of silver into Spain from the mines of Bavaria, which, along with population growth, initiated the inflationary process known as the Price Revolution. The discovery in 1546 of the richest silver mines in the world at Potosi in Bolivia and Zacatecas in Mexico added new momentum to the inflation. Up to the 1560s, output increased along with prices and population. Spain's main export was her famous merino wool, and her major manufacture the high-quality textiles woven from it. This was distributed to the markets of Central and Northern Europe through the great *entrepot* of Antwerp in exchange for timber, naval stores, metals and, when needed, grain. However, ship-building, housing and manufactures for the expanding population of the cities and Atlantic settlements also flourished – up to 1570.

What aborted Spain's development thereafter was her obsession with war. She had to defend not only her Northern border with France but also the vast frontier of the Holy Roman Empire while maintaining internal unity over a territory riven by religious schisms and conflicting regional aspirations. She also had to protect her still-vital Mediterranean trade and interests. Philip II fought the Ottoman navy throughout the 1560s until his decisive victory at the battle of Lepanto (1571). He fought the French in Italy for years before ousting them and adding Sicily, Naples, Milan and Sardinia to his already-unwieldy empire (1559). Not satisfied with vanquishing the French in Italy, he continued military interventions in mainland France in the French Wars of Religion, culminating in a formal Franco-Spanish War (1595–1598). Meanwhile, he had fought and annexed Portugal (1581), along with her Eastern outposts and Brazil. Spain was at war with England from 1585 to 1604, a prolonged belligerency in which the destruction of the Spanish Armada

62 The first industrial nation

(1588), accomplished more by the English weather than the English navy, was just an episode. Above all, there was Spain's protracted and abortive effort to suppress the revolt of the Netherlands, which began in 1568 and consumed most of Spain's resources and Philip's energies. Meanwhile, things were far from tranquil at home. Philip II had to launch his armies against rebels in Navarre, in Aragon and against the Moriscos of Grenada in Alpujarra (1570).

Nor did the death of Philip II and the ascent to power of his successors reduce the military preoccupations of Spain, whether internal or external. Philip III expelled the Moriscos from Spain because of concerns about their possible extraterritorial loyalty to their fellow Muslim Turks, thereby losing a large, skilled and industrious segment of the population. This was not, however, the end of internal dissent. The Basque rebelled in 1634. Catalonia revolted in 1640, inviting France to rule the province until the Catalonians themselves decided that this amounted to jumping from the frying pan into the fire. Portugal declared independence and defeated the Spanish armies sent against them. After a twelve-year truce (1609–1621), Spain resumed her war against the Dutch, drawing in support for the latter from the English and the French. She also fought the French in the Thirty Years War, ending only with the Treaty of Westphalia and her reluctant recognition of Dutch independence (1648).

Spain's location, adjacent to the other great power of continental Europe and on the frontline of Christendom's resistance to Islam, left her no option but to be a warfare state, as befitted her *conquistador* origins. Warfare on this scale and of this intensity required vast resources – so vast, indeed, that even the deluge of American silver proved inadequate. The monarch debased the coinage, adding fuel to the fires of inflation. He borrowed astronomical sums and defaulted whenever his revenues were unequal to the task of debt servicing. Philip II declared bankruptcy four times during his reign. When his sources of credit dried up, as they inevitably did, he had no alternative but to tax his subjects savagely while economizing on infrastructure such as roads and (especially after the expulsion of the Moriscos) irrigation.[5] Manufacturing collapsed under the weight of taxation, cities shrank, agriculture dwindled as its urban market contracted and its irrigation channels dried up. From 1570, Spain's population was in decline. People sought refuge from taxes in the colonies or in the church (thus reducing marriage and birth rates) or, if they could, joined the bloated, corrupt and unproductive bureaucracy. Those who had none of these options simply delayed or avoided marriage and family formation. As population and irrigation contracted, land was switched from arable to pasture because of the latter's lower labour and water requirements. This was strongly encouraged by the state (which legislated repeatedly in favour of the *mesta*, the shepherds' guild) because wool, the chief pastoral product and export, was easy to tax. Unfortunately, this was also the period in which the luxury textiles woven out of Spain's high-quality wool were being priced out of their markets by the lighter, cheaper 'new draperies' made of English wool. The depopulation of Spain not only hit the economy; it also posed problems for military recruitment. Many of Spain's armies were now composed primarily of German mercenaries who were not easily controlled if unpaid. In 1575, for example, Spain's unpaid mercenaries sacked Antwerp so destructively that it lost its commercial importance forever.

By the mid-seventeenth century, Spain's hopes of paramountcy in Europe were a fast-fading memory. Her population was dwindling, her economy was in ruins, her political and military power was being openly defied within and without her territories. Her colonies survived, but their markets were being increasingly catered to by the Dutch, the English and the French. Europe's economic leadership had passed long ago to one of her former subjects, one whose independence she had only just formally recognized.

The eventual failure of the Netherlands

From 1580 to 1670, the European economy was dominated by the Dutch Republic. The Netherlands enjoyed easy access up the Rhine to Central Europe and then via the Alpine passes to Northern Italy. Flanders and Brabant had long exploited this advantage to build a flourishing manufacturing, trading and financial hub centred on Antwerp. Antwerp's major industry was woollen textiles, based on English, and later Spanish, wool, but its role as an *entrepot* and banker in intra-European trade and finance was equally important. When Spain, in its effort to suppress the Dutch Revolt against Philip II, captured and destroyed Antwerp, the Northern Netherlands stepped into the resulting vacuum. The seven provinces of the North shared the locational advantages of Brabant and were even closer to the North Sea, the Atlantic and the intercontinental sea-routes that the Iberians had opened up. Amsterdam replaced Antwerp as the financial and industrial capital of Europe, its banks and woollen manufactures, along with those of Leiden, rapidly filling up the void and its ship-building and maritime commerce soon far exceeding the levels achieved by the Low Countries earlier. The Dutch Republic was committed to the sea on a scale undreamt-of earlier. It is estimated that 10% of all adult males in the Netherlands were sailors and that by 1670, half of Europe's shipping tonnage was Dutch, the size of the Dutch fleet exceeding those of England, Scotland, France, Germany, Spain and Portugal put together. The maritime supremacy of the Dutch was based largely on cheap bulk trades – grain, timber and ship's stores from the Baltic and herring from the North Sea. To transport such freight, they designed a low, flat, unarmed and lightly manned vessel, the *fluyt*, that could easily negotiate the largely peaceful Baltic with a low-value cargo that was unlikely to attract pirates. The consequence: freight rates far lower than anything their rivals could offer. The Dutch effectively undercut all competition as carriers of the Baltic trade (particularly the crucial grain trade) in the years 1580–1620, when population, demand and prices were booming all over Western and Central Europe.

While brilliantly successful in the Baltic, the *fluyt* was far too vulnerable to pirate and enemy attack to operate in the Atlantic or Indian Ocean or even in a Mediterranean overrun by the Algiers pirates. Much stronger construction and heavier armament were necessary in an age when the Portuguese, the Spaniards, the English and the French were transforming their ships into 'floating gun platforms'. This became

64 The first industrial nation

essential after 1620 when the Thirty Years War ravaged Germany, compelling the Dutch to divert their export and reexport trade elsewhere, particularly to the Mediterranean. The Dutch made the necessary adaptations to their naval architecture – well enough, indeed, to oust the Portuguese from the Spice Islands, Malacca, Ceylon and the Malabar coast and replace them as the monopoly purveyors of spices to Europe. In the Atlantic, they established their presence in the trade of West African slaves for Caribbean sugar, while in 1628, the Dutch admiral Piet Heyn captured the entire Spanish silver fleet off Cuba. However, the point was established that the next phase of the struggle for control of the sea would be decided by military success. And it was in this strategic sphere that the fatal positional weakness of the Dutch was exposed and exploited by England.

In 1651, the Protectorate of Oliver Cromwell enacted the first of a series of Navigation Acts that stipulated that all British imports would have to be carried in British ships or in those of the country of origin and all colonial trade would have to be carried in British ships only. Here was a mercantilist restriction designed to apparently protect Britain's carrying trade and her ship-building industry and to specifically target Dutch carrying and ship-building. However, since British freight rates were higher than Dutch, the Navigation Acts increased the cost of all British imports, including the timber and naval stores that were essential inputs of British ship-building. Further, they increased the cost to foreign buyers of British exports and sharpened the attraction of competing Dutch products and reexports. Had the Navigation Acts been peacefully enforced, they may well have been counter-productive. However, they were enforced by the British navy (or British privateers) intercepting Dutch ships at sea and confiscating their cargo – and often the ships themselves – on one pretext or other. War became inevitable. And in a war, the Dutch laboured under the weight of an insuperable geostrategic asymmetry: all their ships (except for the Baltic fleet) had to pass through British waters, while Britain's access to the ocean was independent of the Dutch. In the war of 1652–1654 alone, Britain captured 1700 Dutch 'prizes'. This did not destroy Dutch naval capacity. In June 1667, a Dutch fleet sailed up the Medway, adjacent to the Thames estuary, burnt the bulk of the British navy and towed away its pride, the flagship the *Royal Charles*, in perhaps the greatest naval defeat ever inflicted on Britain, a defeat that ended the Second Anglo-Dutch War. In the Third, in which the English had recruited the French as allies, the four great victories of Admiral de Ruyter thwarted the allies' plans for a successful invasion of the Netherlands. The Dutch were far from lacking in seamanship, morale, military tactics, naval architecture or armament. But the likelihood of hostile interception of Dutch ocean trade with Asia or America hugely increased its cost because of the large convoys that this necessitated. Meanwhile, the Navigation Acts (eagerly emulated by the French), while they hurt England (and France), also struck at the heart of Dutch trade by denying it legal access to the ports of England, France and their colonies worldwide.

While the English added to the cost of Dutch trade through their naval strategy, the French deployed a uniquely French weapon to undermine the demand for it. The generals in this front of the war against the Dutch Republic were the French master chefs and their secret weapon the *haute cuisine*. The evolution of this culinary technology (based on rich butter-and-cream sauces and the substitution of cheap local French herbs for expensive exotic spices) at the hands of great chefs like la Varenne and its adoption by the court of Louis XIV set the fashion for the entire European aristocracy. Since only aristocrats could afford oriental spices anyway, this eroded the major market for spices and set the stage for the lingering death of the spice trade. The VOC, the Dutch East India Company, made the monopolist's cardinal error of trying to raise prices in a declining market by restricting output and so speeded up the consumer's switch to the new cuisine. The fate of the spice trade illustrates the volatility of the demand for luxuries and the fragility of any growth process based on a luxury trade. Eventually, the VOC sought to diversify its operations into other areas and the intra-Asian carrying trade where other European and Asian merchants were already well established and so was forced into a long period of 'profitless growth'.

However, in the Baltic, the Dutch remained impregnable. Their role as distributors of Baltic grain, timber, shipping stores, iron and the like to the rest of Europe and their accumulated reserves of capital and financial skill enabled them to prolong, though not to increase, their prosperity into the eighteenth century. What finally ended Dutch aspirations to global leadership were the military implications of two other geopolitical variables, one minor and the other very major. The minor factor was that the shallow deltaic harbours of the Netherlands admitted only light flat-bottomed vessels like the *fluyt*, while England's deep-water ports could support heavily armed deep-draught men-o'-war. The major factor was Britain's island immunity from land invasion that enabled her to concentrate her energies on the all-important navy, while the Dutch Republic's long land border invited the attention of envious neighbours like the France of Louis XIV and diverted Dutch resources from the sea. At times, indeed, the English and the French pooled their resources to attack the Republic on multiple fronts. By 1650, the Dutch had to maintain a standing army of 100,000; this amounted to 15% of the entire male population, boys as well as men, of the Republic – in addition, of course, to the 10% of adult males who were sailors. Certainly, the demand for military manpower was partly met by an inflow of mercenaries, but it accentuated wage pressures in the labour market and compelled extortionate taxation, which further intensified wage demands,

Essentially, the Dutch were drained by continuous warfare on many fronts and under severe geostrategic disadvantage, by the labour scarcity it induced, the heavy taxation it necessitated and the high wages that resulted. It was this that eroded the rate of profit on investment in the Netherlands, drove down the interest rate and induced a massive exodus of capital, especially to London, culminating, of course, in the occupation of the British throne by a Dutch merchant prince.[6] By the early eighteenth century, the Dutch had abdicated their status as industrial, political and commercial leaders of Western Europe for the role of rentier-financiers.[7]

The failure of Spain to achieve supremacy in the Western world and the eventual eclipse of the Netherlands were both due to the fact that they were indissolubly

66 The first industrial nation

bound to the European mainland and immersed therefore in its continuous land warfare. Much the same was true of France. England, on the other hand, could opt out, as it essentially did under Elizabeth and again during the Thirty Years War. It retained its focus on the sea, on the direction in which the technology of ocean navigation pointed and its yet-unexploited possibilities. These were to unfold over the next 200 years.

England and the Industrial Revolution

England at the end of the seventeenth century was an essentially free market economy in the throes of a food crisis acute enough to arrest – and sometimes to reverse – population growth and a timber crisis severe enough to block industrial expansion. The increased possibility of enclosure of the arable, however, encouraged farmers to experiment with and adopt new tools, techniques, crops and breeding methods that substantially increased the productivity of land and labour. These included the horse-drawn seed drill (Jethro Tull), the wheel-less Dutch plough and new crop rotations involving turnips and clover (instead of fallowing) to feed livestock and rejuvenate the land (Charles Townshend). These innovations hugely increased the productivity of land and deferred the impending Malthusian crisis by at least a century.

The timber crisis was a rather different story. The replacement of wood by coal wherever technologically possible had moderated the consequences of this crisis but had posed a new technological challenge: the deepening of the coal mines as the surface seams were exhausted led to flooding of the mines and necessitated a new technology of drainage. The old air pumps could not raise water from depths of more than 34 feet – the famous Torricelli problem. More powerful pumps based on a new source of energy had to be invented, and the problem was solved by Thomas Newcomen in 1712 through his steam engine, which exploited the coal freely available in the mine to generate the power needed to drain it.

However, in ship-building and in the extraction and purification of iron, the timber scarcity presented a more complex technological problem. In ship-building, indeed, the problem was not solved until the development of the steam-ship 150 years later. But since both these products were indispensable in the age of ocean navigation and maritime warfare, the immediate consequence was large-scale import from forested regions where wood was more abundant and accessible. England bought ships from New England, which resolved her strategic problem – except, of course, during the American War of Independence. More vulnerable strategically on their passage through the easily blockaded Sound were her imports of Baltic iron from Sweden and, later, Russia. In 1709, Abraham Darby developed the coke-smelting technology. But the production of high-quality coke and the refinement of the smelting process that would eliminate enough of the impurities in the ore were as yet in the distant future, so that while Britain could produce its cast-iron at home, it had yet to import its malleable bar iron from Sweden and Russia. Throughout the eighteenth century, as the English economy expanded, the

The first industrial nation **67**

price of wrought iron was driven up, with Sweden exploiting its initial monopoly position. The incentive for research to invent a new method of refining iron was thus sustained. Only with the development of Henry Cort's puddling process in 1784 did the British iron industry's full potential unfold.

Meanwhile, James Watt's condenser improved the efficiency of the Newcomen steam engine enough to make it worth using at sites other than coal mines. Thermal energy could now be tapped by industry in general, all the more since the iron of which the engines were made was increasingly available at home without paying the high transport cost and export duties that Swedish iron had to bear.

The new technology that Darby, Newcomen, Watt and Cort represented has been aptly described by historians (such as Deane,[8] Landes,[9] Mathias,[10] Brinley Thomas[11] and especially Wrigley[12]) as a switch of the energy and material bases of the British economy from the organic to the mineral. Since energy use was no longer limited to renewable sources like human or animal power, wind, water or sun but could tap into the vast subterranean stock of fossil fuels, an immediate acceleration of growth became possible. This was also facilitated by supplementing vegetable sources of materials (wood) by those of mineral origin (metals). The natural resource basis of the economy, which was highly inelastic until the eighteenth century, now appeared to be almost infinitely elastic. 'Intensive' growth – of per capita income – could now replace 'extensive' growth – of output in step with population at best. This, according to these historians, was the essence of the Industrial Revolution. Of course, if the energy or the ores from these subterranean sources were costly to transport, that would link a region's potential for intensive growth to its geological endowment. Coal, for example, is bulky and heavy and loses all its weight during use; coal-using economic development therefore tends to cluster around coalfields.

A contrary view (articulated by Mokyr[13] and McCloskey[14]) is that fossil fuels had little to do with it. They did not accelerate economic growth, nor did they determine its location. Fuel costs accounted for a very small fraction of total costs of production for non-metallurgical industries (such as cotton textiles) and could not therefore have been a decisive consideration. The prime mover of technological progress was the spirit of scientific enquiry released by the Age of Enlightenment; its embodiment in economic growth was the outcome of the new institutional regime created after 1688. The possession of coal did not matter. Countries that didn't have any could have developed substitute sources of power. If the steam engine had never been invented, the scientific and entrepreneurial spirit of eighteenth-century England – Prometheus unbound by the Glorious Revolution – would have ensured that an alternative technology was conjured up.

Perhaps the last word in this debate belongs to Fernihough and O'Rourke,[15] who examine the link between the growth of cities during the Industrial Revolution and the distribution of coalfields all over Europe. They considered the period between 1750 (when coal-using technologies began to penetrate the iron and steel industry and the steam engine was about to be deployed outside coalfields) and 1900 (when alternative forms of energy were making their advent and falling transport costs of

68 The first industrial nation

coal were reducing the value of location on a coalfield). Their results triumphantly vindicated Wrigley et al.: in 1750, the distribution of cities had little to do with the location of coalfields, yet during the period 1750–1900, over 60% of European city growth could be explained by proximity to coal.

An alternative interpretation of the Industrial Revolution is in terms of mechanization – the substitution not of minerals for organic materials and energy sources but of machinery for labour. Mechanization generally implied, of course, the mobilization of capital and more powerful sources of energy, but it also implied higher labour productivity which would support a higher per capita income. The impulse for mechanization was supplied by the emergence of a vast and highly elastic market for cotton textiles and the potential for an almost infinitely elastic supply of the raw material. In the seventeenth century, the East India Company had discovered its alternative to the spice trade from which it had been shut out by the VOC: the calicos of Bengal had been flooding the markets not only of England but also of the rest of Europe, Africa and America – so much so, indeed, that English woollen producers had in 1720 pressured Parliament to pass the Calico Act, which banned not only the import but even the possession of cotton clothing. While the restrictions on the use of cotton cloth were later relaxed to enable a fledgling English cotton textile industry to emerge, the ban on imports remained. However, in markets outside England, Bengal calicoes continued to reign supreme: given the low wages and high skills of the Bengal weavers, it was impossible for cotton textile producers elsewhere to compete under existing technology. The outcome: a powerful incentive for labour-saving innovation in the English cotton textile industry – innovations like Hargreaves' spinning jenny, Arkwright's water-frame and Crompton's mule – devices that could harness the power of running water and later of steam to the spinning of yarn. Meanwhile, beginning in the seventeenth century but really flourishing in the late eighteenth and nineteenth centuries after Eli Whitney's invention of the cotton gin, the American South had become the purveyor of an almost infinitely elastic supply of the raw material across the Atlantic to England's West coast for manufacture in the mills of Manchester and Preston. The consequences were spectacular. By 1860, cotton accounted for 58% of US exports, cotton textiles for 40% of Britain's. One-fifth of Britain's 22 million people were directly or indirectly involved with cotton textiles.[16]

The mechanization of the cotton textile industry and its explosive growth is perhaps the most dramatic episode of the Industrial Revolution. But it is only one example of the general spread of mechanization in eighteenth- and nineteenth-century England. Why did Britain mechanize first, and why, even after the technology of the steam engine and of mechanized spinning became common knowledge, did their adoption in other countries of Europe and Asia lag until many decades later? Allen[17] has shown that this was the consequence of the distinctive configuration of factor prices in eighteenth- and nineteenth-century Britain. Thanks to international trade expansion over centuries, British real wages in the eighteenth century were higher relative to the prices of energy and capital than in any other country. Labour-saving and energy- and capital-intensive techniques were profitable in

Britain long before they became worthwhile anywhere else – which was why they were invented in Britain in the first place.

An interesting aspect of the Industrial Revolution is the role of the four sectors in which revolutionary innovations occurred – cotton textiles, coal, iron and steam – in the general process of British economic growth in the years between 1760 and 1850. The total factor productivity calculations of Crafts and Harley[18] suggest that their contributions (including their immediate linkage effects) to aggregate growth were minimal. Was the synchronization of the spread of these key innovations with the undoubted nineteenth-century spurt in Britain's growth then purely coincidental? We argue that the crucial contribution of the innovating sectors to macroeconomic growth cannot be captured by such calculations because they were essentially externalities. Like foreign trade (the impact of which lasted from the sixteenth to the nineteenth century), they led to urbanization. Coal and (to a lesser extent) iron created the towns in the mining belts. The steam engine not only added to the attraction of these areas (because of the cheap availability of coal) but also favoured agglomeration by increasing the advantages of large factories over small and domestic producers. Cotton textiles gravitated towards Manchester because of (1) water power from fast-flowing Lancashire streams and proximity to coal in the later era of steam and (2) easy access to the raw cotton of the American South and vast export markets worldwide through the port of Liverpool. Since large masses of materials and products had to be moved, the attraction of ports that enabled cheap water transport increased. The proliferation of these towns and the emergence of employment, income and demand at specific nuclei provided markets for, and therefore strongly attracted, industry in general besides strongly stimulating local dairy production and market gardening. The effect was strongest on activities that were not necessarily technologically progressive but were amenable to increasing returns and yielded a product that was not easy to transport. The concentration of industry not only fed cumulatively on itself but also, because of internal and external economies of scale, increased the rate of profit and the incentives to save and invest. Crafts' estimates show gross domestic investment as a proportion of GDP rising from 5.7% in 1760 to 11.7% in 1831.[19] It was the economics of location that hugely magnified the economic consequences of coal, cotton, iron and steam.

What was the contribution of foreign trade to the Industrial Revolution? Opinion is sharply divided between the Dean-Habakkuk-Pomeranz argument that war, trade and mercantilism paved the way for the dramatic transformation of the late eighteenth and nineteenth centuries and the Crafts-Harley–McCloskey thesis that the Industrial Revolution was the home-made product of technological innovation and that 'trade was the child of industry'. The views of the latter school have been bolstered by cliometric calculations that suggest that, given the factor endowments of Britain in 1760, autarchy would have had a minor effect on GDP.

However, technological change was not an autonomous consequence of British ingenuity and institutions. Findlay and O'Rourke[20] have argued that foreign trade ensured large, highly elastic markets and raw material supplies for cotton textiles; this was what created incentives for textile innovations. Allen claims that international

70 The first industrial nation

trade made England a high-wage economy with cheap energy and capital much before the Industrial Revolution and that it was this factor price configuration that led to the cluster of labour-saving and capital- and energy-intensive innovations at the end of the eighteenth century. Trade, in short, created the opportunities for investment and innovation, the technology and the factor endowment that Britain inherited on the eve of the Industrial Revolution. Calculations of the gains from trade under the assumption of given factor endowments and technology are like an enactment of Hamlet without the Prince of Denmark.

Recently, Clark, O'Rourke and Taylor[21] have demonstrated that, while given the factor endowments of 1760, trade added little to Britain's standard of living, the structure of the British economy changed so drastically in the following century that, by 1860, autarchy would have compelled a 25–30% loss in GDP and a major redistribution *à la* Ricardo in favour of landlords. The much larger dependence on foreign trade was a function of a population explosion that far outstripped the capacity of British agriculture and an unbalanced pattern of technological change that increased the productivity of the coal, iron and steel and cotton textile sectors of the economy far more than of the others, thus creating a strong comparative advantage for Britain in these dynamic sectors.

The structural change induced by the Industrial Revolution was, of course, industrialization. The growth of industry, towns and population from 1760 onward generated a huge increase in the demand for food even as agricultural labour supply declined. Some increases in agricultural productivity were indeed achieved through innovations like Coke of Hokeham's selective breeding of high-yielding livestock, but these were quite inadequate since chemical fertilizers were as yet in the distant future, and diminishing returns could not possibly be averted. Food prices sky-rocketed throughout the first quarter of the nineteenth century, driving up wages, eroding profits *à la* Ricardo and spurring violent protests that forced successive extensions of the franchise, culminating in adult suffrage. A part of this process of progressive retreat by the landed gentry who had earlier dominated Parliament was the repeal of the Corn Laws which had, until 1846, restricted the import of food. After the repeal, English markets were flooded with cheaper grain, from Germany, Poland and Russia in the short run and from the New World in the long. The expanding demand of industrializing England and Western Europe for food drove transport innovations like the railway, the steam ship, refrigeration and the like. Their rapid spread enabled the settlement and development of the American frontier. A new pattern of international specialization began to unfold, with America exporting food and raw materials to England and importing her manufactures. While this resolved England's Ricardian problem and revived the momentum of her industrialization in the mid-nineteenth century, it permanently destroyed her agriculture. From 1873, when the wheat of the Great Plains first hit the European market, agricultural prices and incomes collapsed; so did agricultural demand for manufactures, triggering a depression that lasted the rest of the century. This was the beginning of the end of Britain's industrial hegemony, sometimes, but controversially, described as her climacteric.

America and Britain's climacteric

England's 'climacteric' was largely a matter of *relative* decline as the growth of the United States, Germany and Russia accelerated. All three were great continental countries, and the change in the relative pace of growth between them and the European maritime fringe represented a shift in the relative balance of economic activity and power between the sea and the land that reversed the process that began with the ocean voyages of the fifteenth and sixteenth centuries. To illustrate this shift, we touch briefly on the dramatic story of US industrialization in the second half of the nineteenth century. The late nineteenth century was an age of transport innovations that, in scale and intensity, matched the sixteenth-century era of ocean navigation. It witnessed not only the railway revolution (borrowing a technology developed in England in the 1820s) but also the internal combustion engine (which harnessed the other great fossil fuel of the modern world to the needs of land and air transport), the steam ship and refrigeration (which increased the portability of perishables). The nineteenth-century spurt of innovation was set off by the pressure of rapid industrialization on the limited natural resource base of the European maritime periphery. It was common knowledge that the vast virgin resources of the New World awaited exploitation if a technology of mass access could be developed. Since the end of the Napoleonic blockades in 1815, an almost unlimited supply of American raw cotton was available at Liverpool for transport to the Lancashire mills and transformation into cloth, which in turn had to be moved to Liverpool for export to a vast international market. It was in this milieu that Stephenson and other engineers developed the railway locomotive. The rapid adoption and development of this English invention followed immediately after the repeal of the Corn Laws. With demand for food shooting up in the England of the Hungry Forties, settlement, cultivation and large-scale grain export raced across the United States and Canadian prairies on the track of the railroad. With steam engine technology delivering increasingly light and mobile engines, it could be applied to water transport, first to unify the great river valleys of the American interior, then to accelerate trans-Atlantic carriage in step with the railway. As America diversified from arable to pasture, the speeding up of transport was supplemented by refrigeration technology, which made possible the export of frozen meat not just across the Atlantic but eventually from sources as distant as Australia and New Zealand. Meanwhile, more intensive exploration of the natural resource endowment of America widened the range of her primary exports from plantation products and grain to meat, minerals and timber.

The growth of population and income in the New World, as indeed in the continental areas of Europe, created a local demand for market-oriented manufactures that led to industrial development and urbanization, particularly around ports, railway hubs and mining belts. Urbanization in turn generated demand for a new mode of land transport which could be personalized, a mode that offered freedom and flexibility about times, routes and destinations. Horses offered these advantages in earlier transport regimes, but maintaining a horse – leave alone a horse-drawn

72 The first industrial nation

carriage – in a congested city was a luxury that only the very rich could possibly dream of. Bicycles were the poor man's alternative. But the less energetic wanted a personal machine powered by a source much lighter than any steam engine. This was the motivation behind the prolonged search for a workable internal combustion engine, a search that led to Nikolaus Otto's engine and Karl Benz's complete automobile. As with many other innovations, while this German invention did indeed benefit Germany, the major beneficiary was the United States. Her rapidly growing towns and vast area requiring a fine network of roads to encircle and feed the railway stations supplied the ideal environment for the growth of automobile travel, especially after the discovery of the country's immense oil reserves. This was further accentuated by her adoption of yet another German innovation, Rudolf Diesel's modification of the petrol engine to accommodate a cheaper fuel that could drive trucks, locomotives, ships and all kinds of machinery, including agricultural equipment.

While these innovations were primarily in the field of transport, urbanization also paved the way for a crucial general-purpose technology: electricity. After Edison's electric bulb and Tesla's alternating current helped light up cities by transmission of electricity from central power stations, a vast field of applications of the new form of energy opened up. Factories began electrifying their machinery. A demand emerged for a whole host of electrically powered domestic appliances, spawning large new industries. New modes of long-distance communication and entertainment such as the telephone and the radio became possible. With street-cars, subways and street lighting, electricity became an essential part not only of household life but also of urban public infrastructure, all of which led to an exponential growth of urban industrial demand with consequent external and internal economies of scale.

A major determinant of the size of the market for manufactures was the real wage level. In America, outside the South, the high land/man ratio ensured a high real wage. The bulk of the population earned enough of a surplus over their subsistence needs to buy manufactures: as the economy expanded, industrial demand rose more than proportionally, and since many manufactures were market-oriented, this stimulated local industrialization. In the Southern states, wages had been forced down before the Civil War by the presence of a huge army of slaves. After the Civil War, large numbers of them remained locked in their existing locations because they were too poor to migrate. The South remained an unequal society polarized between a handful of rich planters who were too few and a mass of low-wage labour which was too poor to constitute a large market for any manufacture: the plantation economy offered no escape route to industrialization.

The sheer size of the US economy and the high level of wages soon made it the world's largest industrial market. US industry in the mid-nineteenth century still required and received protection to offset its high wage costs. A crucial factor here was the defeat of the Confederacy in the Civil War, which tilted the balance of political power strongly against the plantation-based export economies of the South which were staunch advocates of free trade. By the end of the century, however, scale economies in the vast US market neutralized any labour cost disadvantages, and US manufacturers were challenging British supremacy in most third-country markets, even without the benefits of protection.

The size of the economy also constituted the major incentive for research, and the high wage rate gave the resulting innovations a strongly labour-saving bias. Of course, despite the Patent Acts, the fruits of research rapidly became common knowledge. However, the right of seigniorage (first use) itself conferred significant profits: this was especially so because, in the early experimental stages of an invention, the research scientist, the production engineer and the market analyst had to work in close cooperation to iron out the glitches that inevitably appear at that time.

All this combined to give US industrialization an explosive momentum that enabled it to overtake Britain by the outset of the First World War.

The industrial development of Germany lagged slightly behind that of the United States and, like that of the latter, owed much to the railway revolution in opening up its interior. Railway construction in the 1830s and 1840s added to the traditional advantages of Prussia and Poland in exporting grain to Britain. Along with the economic unification of Germany (because of the Zollverein customs union and the political unification achieved later by Bismarck), the railways facilitated the exploitation of the immense coal and iron reserves of North West Germany (including Alsace, seized from France in 1871). But by the 1870s, as railways penetrated deeper into the emptier and more fertile American prairies and the Russian black earth steppe, Prussia could no longer compete internationally with American or Russian grain, and German economic development became increasingly focused on industrialization centred on the coal and iron of the Ruhr. Coal technology yielded significant by-products (such as dyes) and stimulated the development of German chemistry and the chemical industry. Germany also, of course, pioneered the development of automobile technology, contributing thereby to the revolution in land transport.

The industrial development of Russia lagged even further behind but, like that of Germany and the United States, was based on the railway revolution opening up the interior of a vast landmass with its wealth of agricultural resources, metals and fossil fuels that could not be tapped earlier due to the backwardness of land transport. In all three cases, despite the enormous differences in institutions and historical heritage, we have a process driven by the interaction of geography and current technology. Institutions and history no doubt account for the lags in the process and the very different paths taken by the three countries to economic progress, but there can be little doubt that the impact of the land transport revolution on countries with broadly similar geography explains their rapid economic growth in the late nineteenth and twentieth centuries. It was the contrast of this dynamism with the relative stagnation of Britain that led to the perception of a British climacteric. By the end of the Second World War, Britain had resigned herself to the economic and political realities of the new world order, dismantled an empire she could no longer afford and accepted her position as a distinctly junior partner in the Anglo-American alliance, an alliance prompted largely by her recognition that she could no longer possibly cope by herself with adversaries like Germany or Russia.

74 The first industrial nation

Notes

1 J. U. Nef, The Progress of Technology and the Growth of Large Scale Industry in Great Britain, 1540–1640, *Economic History Review*, 1st series, 5 (1), 1934, pp. 3–24.

2 S. Broadberry et al., *British Economic Growth 1270–1870*, Cambridge: Cambridge University Press, 2015, ISBN 1107070783, Chapter 1, and Table 5.06, p. 205.

   See also E. A. Wrigley, R. S. Schofield, *The Population History of England, 1541–1871: A Reconstruction*, Cambridge, MA: Harvard University Press, 1981, Table 7.8, pp. 208–209, [1].

3 D. W. Waters, *The Art of Navigation in England in Elizabethan and Early Stuart Times*, London: Hollis and Carter, 1958.

4 D. W. Waters, *The Iberian Bases of the English Art of Navigation in the Sixteenth Century*, 1970.

5 D. O. Flynn, Fiscal Crisis and the Decline of Spain (Castile), *Journal of Economic History*, 42 (1), 1982, pp. 139–147.

6 C. Wilson, The Economic Decline of the Netherlands, *Economic History Review*, 9 (2), 1939, pp. 111–159.

   C. Wilson, Cloth Production and International Competition in the Seventeenth Century, *Economic History Review*, 13 (2), 1960, pp. 209–221.

   C. Wilson, Taxation and the Decline of Empires, in C. Wilson (ed.), *Economic History and the Historian*, 1969.

7 J. de Vries, A. van der Woude, *The First Modern Economy: Success, Failure, and Perseverance of the Dutch Economy, 1500–1815*, Cambridge: Cambridge University Press, 1997.

8 P. Deane, *The First Industrial Revolution*, Cambridge: Cambridge University Press, 1979.

9 D. Landes, *The Unbound Prometheus: Technological Change and Industrial Development in Western Europe from 1750 to the Present*, Cambridge and New York: Press Syndicate of the University of Cambridge, 1969.

10 P. Mathias, *The First Industrial Nation: An Economic History of Britain 1700–1914*, London: Routledge, 1969.

11 B. Thomas, *The Industrial Revolution and the Atlantic Economy*, London: Routledge, 1993.

12 E. A. Wrigley, *The Path to Sustained Growth: England's Transition from an Organic Economy to an Industrial Revolution*, Cambridge: Cambridge University Press, 2016.

13 J. Mokyr, *A Culture of Growth: The Origins of the Modern Economy*, Princeton: Princeton University Press, 2016.

14 D. McCloskey, *Bourgeois Equality: How Ideas, Not Capital or Institutions, Enriched the World*, Chicago: University of Chicago Press 2016.

15 A. Fernihough, K. H. O'Rourke, *Coal and the European Industrial Revolution*, NBER Working Paper 19802, 2014.

16 G. Dattel, The South's Mighty Gamble on King Cotton, *American Heritage Magazine*, 2010.

17 R. C. Allen, Technology and the Great Divergence: Global Economic Development since 1820, *Explorations in Economic History*, 49, 2012, pp. 1–16.

18 N. F. R. Crafts, *British Economic Growth during the Industrial Revolution*, Oxford: Clarendon Press, 1985.

   N. F. R. Crafts, C. K. Harley, Output Growth and the Industrial Revolution, *Economic History Review*, 45 (4), 1992, pp. 703–730.

19 N. E. R. Crafts, British Economic Growth, 1760–1831, *Economic History Review*, IInd series, 36 (2), 1983, pp. 177–199.

20 R. Findlay, K. H. O'Rourke, *Power and Plenty: Trade, War and the World Economy in the Second Millennium*, Princeton: Princeton University Press, 2001.

21 G. Clark, K. H. O'Rourke, A. M. Taylor, The Growing Dependence of Britain on Trade during the Industrial Revolution, *The Scandinavian Economic History Review*, 62 (2), 2014, pp. 109–136.

6

FULL CIRCLE[1]

The 'fixed characteristics' of countries that we have portrayed as interacting with technological change have, up to this point, been their natural, primarily geographical, features. But as the progress of science has reduced the importance of natural constraints, as, for example, innovations in transport and communications have annihilated distance, man-made factors have come to the fore in defining the 'fixed characteristics' of a country. The most important of these are migration restrictions. Migration restrictions represent man-made labour immobilities that perpetuate differences in population density between countries and tend to create differences in labour cost. In the world of the late twentieth and early twenty-first centuries, where technology has made goods, capital and data almost perfectly mobile, trade patterns were now determined largely by these labour cost differentials. Low-wage economies were attracting manufacturing, initially of labour-intensive goods but later also of capital-intensive products with a standardized technology like cars and steel (since capital too had become highly mobile). Their manufactures began flooding world markets, displacing manufacturers based in the advanced West. Western comparative advantage was reduced to the high-tech research-intensive industries on the frontiers of technology, and there, the public good character of the knowledge generated by these industries was a major deterrent to investment. Labour demand, wages and growth shot up in densely populated Asia, while they stagnated over the long term in the West. With Asian resurgence and the decline of the West, the wheel of fortune had, it seemed, turned full circle since the beginnings of ocean navigation and trade in the sixteenth and seventeenth centuries. This process – and its consequences delineated in this chapter – account for the most recent, indeed the contemporary, episode of our story.

The reversal of fortune of the late twentieth century

For the better part of the twentieth century, global wealth and power remained concentrated in the Western world, in North America and Europe, with the other continents trailing far behind. There were, of course, shifts in the internal balance of power and pelf within the Euro-American world, the eclipse of Britain, the dominance of the United States, the increasing importance of Germany and Russia, but, except for the isolated aberration of post-Meiji Japan, the rest of the world, so it seemed, could never hope to reach the portals of the club of rich nations, let alone challenge their hegemony.

From the mid-1960s, however, things began to change, gradually at first, but accelerating dramatically from the seventies. It began with four countries on the Asian rim of the Pacific, South Korea, Taiwan and the city states of Hong Kong and Singapore, that erupted on the world market of the late sixties and seventies with an explosion of manufactured exports powering spurts of growth unmatched in living memory. The economics profession remained sceptical. Joan Robinson, savant of the Cambridge left, declared that Korea and Taiwan owed their brief prosperity to massive injections of US aid, while Hong Kong and Singapore were too small to count. However, as time passed and US aid tapered off, there was little sign of deceleration in Korea and Taiwan. Meanwhile, the Asian Tigers, as they christened themselves, were succeeded by the NICs. These newly industrializing countries, Thailand, Malaysia and Indonesia, followed closely the trajectory of the pioneers with large-scale exports of manufactures as the spearhead of rapid growth. And at the end of the decade of the 1970s, China, after the death of Chairman Mao, joined the East Asian bandwagon of fast-growing industrial exporters. China's initial steps, of course, deviated from the typical pattern of East Asian growth, as they involved a correction of the course set by the Great Helmsman for the erstwhile Communist nation: many sectors of industry and commerce were opened up to private enterprise; the communes that had been imposed on Chinese agriculture in the 1960s were effectively dissolved, stimulating agricultural incentives so potently that in the six years 1978–1984, the per capita income of rural China doubled and large volumes of rural savings were generated and labour released for deployment in industry. Thereafter, China's industrialization accelerated and her manufactures began flooding markets worldwide. A decade or so later, the other major centre of the world's population, South Asia, joined the Asian enterprise, by now well established, of rapid growth propelled by industrial exports. So did the smaller, erstwhile socialist economy of Vietnam.

The rates of growth achieved by East and South Asia were historically unprecedented. Meanwhile, however, the advanced West, and Asia's lone industrial pioneer, Japan, sank into stagnation. Demand for labour shrank, employment and real wages stagnated or declined, industries disappeared and growth rates collapsed. Remarkably, chronic economic stagnation coexisted with spectacular scientific and technological progress in the West, while in East Asia, the contribution of technological change to her astronomical economic growth was assessed by economists (like Alwyn Young[2] and Lawrence Lau[3]) as negligible. Princeton economist and Nobel Laureate Paul Krugman[4] famously claimed in the 1990s that, since the Tiger economies were merely emulating the technologies of the West and not generating any of their own, their high growth rates were simply a function of their technological lag: as they caught up, the momentum of their growth would die out. Indeed, he claimed that 'the Asian debacle' of 1997 signalled the end of Asia's growth story. As it turned out, the obituary was premature. So were similar prophecies of doom that accompanied the crisis of 2008. Asian growth revived and continues at a rapid pace today.

The stage is therefore set for another 'reversal of fortune', in rates of growth if not yet in levels of income, perhaps at least for a 'great convergence'. Will Asia, which dominated the world in the sixteenth century before lapsing into disastrous backwardness, recover some of its glory, if not its dominance? And what accounts for the extraordinary transition that we have already witnessed, a transition that runs totally counter to the geographical distribution of technological progress? We seek in this chapter to explore these questions.

Transport and the international trade theory of the reversal of fortune

A crucial issue is the role of transport cost in this process. In a world of perfect mobility, differences between nations and regions in prices, wages, rates of profit and per capita incomes would be instantly erased by arbitrage of goods and factors of production. It is transport cost that separates national and regional markets and economies, legitimizes comparisons between them and makes it possible to trace reversals of fortune. Barriers between economies can be either natural or manmade. In earlier chapters, we have underlined the importance of transport innovations in differentially reducing barriers to the movement of goods and people across different environments and thereby moderating differences in the relative economic performance of different nations and regions. Of course, they reduce natural, not man-made, barriers. And man-made barriers to the large-scale movement of people are often more refractory than those to the movement of goods. In earlier times, such barriers often had to be overcome by invasion, except when the recipient country was empty or its resistance had already been crushed by force of arms – as with the flow of European migrants to the New World between the sixteenth and nineteenth centuries. Today, though illegal migration has not ceased, migration restrictions are enforced strictly enough for the assumption of international labour immobility to be a reasonable approximation to reality.

If capital is also internationally immobile, each country can be characterized by its factor endowment. The capital-abundant countries would tend to have higher wages and lower returns to capital before trade (assuming that demand patterns are not too different internationally). Capital-intensive goods would tend to have lower unit costs and therefore relatively lower prices in such economies – and would therefore be exported by them once trade is opened. In contrast, labour-abundant

78 Full circle

countries would export labour-intensive goods. This was the content of the Factor Endowments Hypothesis[5] developed by Swedish economists Eli Heckscher and Bertil Ohlin to explain the pattern of international trade.

Trade, moreover, would change factor prices. Producers of capital-intensive goods in capital-abundant countries would experience an increase in demand through exports, thus supporting a rise in the price of capital. Labour-intensive goods in labour-abundant countries would witness a rise in demand and prices, inducing a rise in demand for labour and therefore in wages. Factor prices would tend to converge relative to their autarchy levels. However, if factor prices are not quite equalized, capital-abundant countries would persist with lower returns to capital and higher wages than labour-abundant countries. Such were the predictions of the Factor Price Equalization Theorem[6] propounded by the first Nobel laureate in economics, Paul Samuelson of MIT.

Now, if free capital mobility is permitted, capital would flow from capital-rich countries to capital-poor ones until factor prices were equalized. Factor price equalization would sharply reduce per capita income inequalities between nations. The only source of international income inequalities would now be disparities in factor endowment, which also would have been substantially reduced – though not necessarily eliminated – by capital flows from capital-abundant to labour-abundant countries.

Theory and reality

Or so one thought. And so did the neoclassical theory of international trade predict.[7] But, at least until the 1960s, the predictions bore little resemblance to the reality. There was little evidence until then that the rate of profit on capital was higher in poor countries than in rich ones, nor was there a massive exodus of capital from the rich to the poor countries. The bulk of international investment flowed from rich countries to other rich countries. Since the mainspring of the process did not work, its outcome was never realized. Factor prices were never equalized, nor did per capita incomes converge.

Why did the conclusions of international trade theory diverge so sharply from reality? The logic of the theory was iron-clad. The problem lay in its assumptions – in particular the assumptions of perfect mobility of goods and constant returns to scale. Perfect commodity mobility implied a single unified world market in which any good traded at a uniform price worldwide. Constant returns to scale meant that profitability depended only on relative factor prices and not at all on scales of production. Together, the two assumptions made the location of industry essentially independent of the location of the market.

Neither of the two crucial assumptions corresponded to the realities of the twentieth century. Far-from-negligible costs of transport and communication – apart, of course, from trade restrictions – splintered the world market into regional and national segments. And increasing returns were a pervasive fact of industrial life at least until the 1960s. Economies of scale were a huge boon to manufacturers based in large markets, enabling them to overcome the hurdle of possibly higher wages. Producers located in small markets could achieve such scale economies only by invading large markets abroad, thus incurring high distribution cost. Typically, large industrial markets existed in rich capital-abundant countries. In poor, densely populated economies, the market for manufactures was restricted by three distinct factors. First, low GDP set an outside limit to the size of the market. Second, low per capita income meant that only a small proportion of this low GDP was spent on manufactures in accord with Engel's Law, one of the most widely accepted empirical generalizations in all of economics. Third, income in densely populated poor countries is generally very unequally distributed. The low returns to labour (the one resource that is universally owned in a non-slave society) and the high returns to property (which is highly concentrated in a few hands) lead to a society polarized between a microscopic elite and a mass of the very poor. The poor are too poor to buy any but the most basic necessities. The rich, on the other hand, are too few to constitute a large market for any single product: they buy a large variety rather than a substantial quantity of any one thing. Thus, mass markets for manufactures are even more limited than one would expect from the value of per capita income.

In consequence, manufacturers based in poor countries, despite their lower wage costs, could not effectively compete with rich country producers – because in most industries, the scale consideration outweighed relative factor costs in determining profitability. There were exceptions, of course – very highly labour-intensive industries (such as cotton textiles), industries not amenable to standardization and mass production (such as handicrafts), industries with negligible transport cost. But for the overwhelming bulk of manufactures, the potential comparative advantage of poor low-wage economies was nullified by diseconomies of small scale.

In primary production, on the other hand, countries with high land/man ratios had a comparative advantage not only because of cheap arable land for agriculture but also because the larger the surface area, the higher the probability of specific geographic advantages such as mineral content or specific types of climate or topography. The densely populated poor countries could not compete with richer rivals in manufacturing – or with the thinly populated countries in primary production. They therefore remained peripheral players in the world economy.

The rehabilitation of theory

From the sixties, however, changes in technology, in the nature of the market, in the distribution of worldwide wealth and in the world trading regime reduced the importance of transport costs and economies of scale in world trade.

- A long-term process of gradual dismantling of trade barriers began with the Kennedy Round in the sixties and culminated eventually in the establishment of the World Trade Organization (WTO).
- Technological changes included containerization and deep-draught freighters that reduced shipping costs, the information technology revolution that mini-

80 Full circle

mized communication and information costs and 'just-in-time' management technology which eliminated warehousing and storage. The increased uncertainty of a globalized business environment prompted other changes in technology: businesses tended to discard fixed equipment (which created long runs of cheaply mass-produced goods but committed firms rigidly to particular products and processes) in favour of 'flexible specialization' based on electronically controlled multipurpose tools that could be adapted at a moment's notice to entirely different methods and products.

- As incomes rose worldwide, demand became increasingly sophisticated. Quality, exclusiveness and variety became major concerns for the consumer rather than mere cheapness (which is what large-scale technology could deliver). There was an increased preference for high-value goods whose material content (and therefore transport cost) was low relative to their prices.

- Finally, the geography of world affluence changed: the world's wealth was redistributed from a primarily North Atlantic locus to the Middle East (because of the oil price explosion of the 1970s) and the Pacific (because of the rapid growth first of Japan and California in the fifties and sixties and then of the Asian Tigers). This geographic dispersion of global wealth made the rich markets of the world accessible to the poorer countries at lower transport costs.

The improvements in transport and communication technology annihilated distance. They reduced drastically the importance of natural barriers to the movement of goods, money and people worldwide. They did not, however, eliminate man-made barriers. While the movement towards free trade and the emergence of the WTO reduced some of these, migration restrictions remained most intractable. As goods and other resources became relatively mobile, the labour force became the most distinctive feature of any country's environment, the one that determined its success in adapting to current technology. And technology itself was changing in a way that made the relatively fixed features of the country's factor endowment more relevant than the scale of production.

An interesting digression that reinforces our general point is related to the late twentieth-century improvements in communication technology. These had two crucial consequences. First, they created networks of information and communication and powered the explosive growth of web-based services. The network externalities thus generated conferred specific advantages on dense populations that could form the basis of dense networks. Second, movement of financial capital became instantaneous and costless: apart from man-made restrictions, capital became perfectly mobile worldwide.

In terms of the Heckscher-Ohlin-Samuelson model, as the importance of transport costs and scale economies dwindled, the conditions necessary for Factor Price Equalization were gradually approximated – and the theorem was increasingly fulfilled. Labour-intensive manufacturing migrated to East and South Asia, creating the Asian Miracle, while the capital-abundant West and Japan concentrated on increasingly capital-intensive industries, ultimately specializing in those with a very high human- and physical-capital content, the research-intensive knowledge industries. Wages rose all over Asia but more rapidly in countries with small populations than in those with large labour surpluses. In Asia, the process of export-led industrialization began in the small countries on the Pacific rim because of two reasons: (1) cheap access over water to what were, in the sixties, the fastest-growing markets of the advanced world, Japan and California, and (2) small size that made it evident to policy-makers that a closed-economy approach to development would be futile and facilitated the opening of the economy. However, the momentum of the growth of manufactured exports soon fully absorbed the labour forces of the four Tigers, driving up their wages and inducing a further migration of labour-intensive manufacturing to countries as yet unexplored by it, particularly those with large labour surpluses, to the NICs, China and South Asia.

Meanwhile, in the West, the return to capital rose, while the demand for and return to labour stagnated, giving rise to long-term economic recession and unemployment despite high profits. The prosperity enjoyed by Asia was not shared to the same degree by Africa or Latin America because the comparative advantage of the latter lay not in labour-intensive but in natural resource-intensive production. Much of the economic history of the last fifty years is explained by this process.

The Asian Miracle

As the new international division of labour unfolded in Asia, per capita incomes increased in the countries that embraced it, stimulating domestic savings as well as investment opportunities. Supplemented by the inflow of foreign capital (wherever this was permitted), it changed factor proportions, prices and production structures in ways that had been predicted in 1955 by Polish-born British economist Tadeusz Rybczynski.[8] Countries where capital grew rapidly (such as the pioneers in the Asian Miracle) gradually lost their comparative advantage in labour-intensive production to others that had lagged behind and switched to relatively less labour-intensive activities. This explains the sequence in which industrialization spread in Asia: the original Gang of Four (Korea, Taiwan, Hong Kong and Singapore) lost their most labour-intensive industries to the NICs (Thailand, Malaysia and Indonesia), and these in turn were followed by Vietnam and, eventually, by China, India and the rest of the subcontinent. This was the 'flying geese' pattern observed and poetically described by Japanese economist Kaname Akamatsu[9] and misattributed by him to the emulation of the technological example of Japan, the lead 'goose', by its East Asian followers.

As wages rose in the Pacific pioneers, blunting their competitive edge in labour-intensive manufacturing relative to their lower-wage neighbours, the pioneers graduated to more capital-intensive industry. This was the sector of the older, well-established industries of the Western world, industries with a mature stabilized technology (such as steel and automobiles) which had long played a part in the Japanese economy. Korea, for example, abandoned men's clothing, wigs and plywood in the late seventies and early eighties to focus increasingly on cars, ship-building and steel,

82 Full circle

activities in which its wages, though substantially higher than in the sixties, still constituted a decisive advantage over the United States and Western Europe. The West, priced gradually out of these traditional manufactures, had no option but to concentrate ever more on research-intensive industries at the frontiers of technology. As products and technology in these frontier industries were standardized, as they switched, as it were, from the frontier to the interior, they were adopted by the East Asians, and the West had to seek fresh pastures further afield.

As Raymond Vernon[10] saw it, the process could be described as a life-cycle through which new products typically passed. Most new products were developed and initially produced where large potential markets existed for them. This meant generally countries with high per capita incomes where consumers and producers had already exhausted the possibilities of older products and were now in quest of novelty. In the experimental phases of a new product, close, perhaps face-to-face, interaction was necessary between the marketing specialist, the production engineer and the research scientist to iron out the initial glitches in the design or the production process. This called for a strong locational linkage between the market, the shop floor and the research laboratory. Rich countries therefore had a comparative advantage in the new product and the technology that produced it. As the product matured, as the more obvious improvements in its design or production process were completed, its technology became standardized. Production could now be separated from the market to which it catered or the research lab that invented it. The costs of production, in particular the labour costs, began now to matter more for the location of the industry. Old producers could relocate to cheaper, lower-wage regions. New producers in these regions could replicate the now-familiar technology if the patent on it had expired or invent around it if it had not. Meanwhile, the pioneering country, having lost its comparative advantage in this product, would have to move on to newer horizons. Vernon's product cycle reinforced the advantage that cheap labour conferred on the Asians in attracting not only labour-intensive but also traditional capital-intensive industries with standardized technology.

While Asian industrialization was set off largely by the wide wage differential between Asia and the West, it had two other crucial requirements. The development of industry, particularly industry with substantial internal and external economies of scale, implied agglomeration and therefore urbanization. Industrialization itself – as well as urbanization – requires a set of public goods – power, roads, a transport and communication network, sanitation, water supply, civic hygiene and public health. Typically, industrialization also requires a labour force literate enough to acquire and absorb new industrial skills. Basic education is therefore a key imperative. All these can be supplied only by a state that assumes a positive role in the whole process. It will, of course, have an incentive to do so because of the revenue potential of the new industries. If, however, it is dominated by an elite committed to the status quo, the state will be sluggish in providing the infrastructure that the new industries require. The past will then act as a drag on the process of industrialization, though the onward march of history should prove eventually to be irresistible.

The expansion of labour-intensive industrialization in Asia and the consequent rise of labour incomes also meant an increase in the demand for food. Had agricultural output not risen in step, food prices would have shot up, driving up wages, eroding the rate of profit and precipitating a Ricardian crisis. The emergence of the new international division of labour would have been summarily aborted. The momentum of the process was sustained by a major technological transformation of agriculture. From 1965 on, the Green Revolution rapidly increased world food supplies and was supplemented as the century wore on by the fruits of an explosion of biogenetic research.

The sequencing of the Miracle: China's short and India's long lag

Why did the Asian Miracle follow the precise geographical sequence that it did? Part of the answer has already been touched upon: the vast and – in the sixties – fast-growing markets of Japan and California accessible by cheap water transport over the Pacific and the relative smallness of the economies of the pioneering Tigers that compelled them to seek markets in the outside world. But it was not just the leads of the leaders but also the lags of the laggards that call for an explanation. In particular, why did those two great reservoirs of surplus labour, China and India, not respond sooner to the opportunities that were seized so gleefully by the Gang of Four?

The answer to this question lies in the durability of the political and economic institutions that these countries inherited from their past. Until the mid-1970s, China had, of course, been an uncompromisingly socialist economy with agriculture ruled by huge communes and industry entirely owned by the state, an economy hermetically sealed away from the allurements of Western capitalism. However, it was also a personal dictatorship with an immense concentration of power in the hands of the dictator. When one dictator died, and a far more pragmatic successor was installed, he legitimately inherited all this power so that policy reversal was relatively smooth and easy. It was all the smoother and easier because the success of the Gang of Four right on China's doorstep was so spectacularly visible to China, better, indeed, than to the rest of the world and because, in three of the Four, the entrepreneurs who led the transformation were expatriate Chinese. The transformation began with agriculture where the household responsibility system effectively replaced the communes with virtual peasant ownership. This started as a grassroots movement in the provinces of Fujian and Anhwei, but soon, with the approval of Deng Xiaoping and the 1981 Plenum of the party, became a deluge that enveloped all of China. The resulting explosion in agricultural productivity, output, income and savings and the large-scale release of labour from food production led to the opening up of rural – and indeed urban – industry to private enterprise, including overseas Chinese enterprise, and, soon after, to foreign investors as well. Market pricing rapidly replaced the administered prices of the past. The state, however, retained monopoly control of basic capital goods industry and infrastructure, which it financed by drawing upon China's astronomically high savings rate. However, it was her labour-intensive light industry that, as with the rest of East Asia, powered her capture of the world market and paved the way for her subsequent entry into rather more capital-intensive fields.

While the imperial authority exercised by Chairman Mao enabled China to ignore the economic revolution occurring on her doorstep and among overseas Chinese for a decade and a half, the vestiges of that authority retained by his successor partly accounted for the rapidity of the catch-up. India's case was very different. In sharp contrast to China's social homogeneity and authoritarian political structure, India was a stable democracy operating in a highly heterogeneous society essentially through compromises between its innumerable interest groups. And powerful interest groups implied powerful vested interests that protected the status quo and resisted change. The Indian case, therefore, is a remarkable study in the evolution in pre-1965 India of interests and institutions that retarded adaptation to the changed world of the last third of the twentieth century.

India's economic regime during the first two decades after Independence was based on export pessimism, the firm belief that the world market, particularly in manufacturing, was inaccessible to her. This belief was nurtured and repeatedly confirmed by experience before the mid-1960s, as described and explained in more general terms in the section 'Theory and Reality'. Yet she was driven down the path of development by population growth and rising aspirations, fuelled by prolonged exposure over 200 years of colonial history to the Western world. Persistence in blissful poverty was simply not an option. The Indian response to this situation was import-substituting industrialization (ISI). Industrial investment in India, it was believed, was deterred by a lack of incentives, a low rate of profit due to inability to compete with rich country manufacturers whether at home or abroad. India, therefore, should develop like a closed economy, with basic heavy industry and infrastructure created by the state and private manufacturers replacing imported consumer goods. The problem of limited industrial markets and low profitability would be solved by a strategy that involved four distinct strands, not all explicitly articulated.

- The rate of profit in industry was raised through a battery of protective devices and subsidies.
- Government demand was injected at strategic points in the economy, with a maximum of locationally associated backward and forward linkages. Railway building, for example, supported the demand for iron and steel, heavy engineering and coal-mining while reducing procurement and distribution costs for all products.
- A large homogeneous middle-class market was created through a vast expansion of government employment – sprawling bureaucracies, large standing armies, huge university establishments and the like.
- Through a series of five-year plans, the government sought to signal to the private sector the areas in which it could expect a future increase in demand,

thus achieving a synchronization of investment plans such that expansion in different fields could support each other.

This was a growth model over which the shadow of the government loomed large, though its actual presence was limited by low income which translated into low taxable capacity. Government was to control what Pandit Nehru picturesquely described as 'the commanding heights of the economy', the basic industries and infrastructure, including not only railway building but also aviation, ship-building, electricity, steel, coal, petroleum, minerals, cement, fertilizers, large-scale irrigation, post and telecommunications and a host of other fields. It was also to control higher education and research. It would decide on tariffs, quotas, subsidies and licences for private business and, of course, on the contracts the latter might receive for government work. It would delineate priorities for investment and affect thereby the fortunes of private investors and producers. It would increase astronomically in size, justifying its growth not in the terms we have set out previously but as a consequence of the vast expansion of the role that it had assigned to itself.

The increase in functions and size of the government implied a vast increase in the discretionary authority of bureaucrats and politicians and therefore in their opportunities for personal enrichment. It also gave private individuals, firms and groups a strong incentive for 'rent-seeking', for lobbying bureaucrats and politicians in order to influence their decisions; in the process, these individuals, firms and groups would divert resources from productive activities (like investment and innovation) to rent-seeking, thus reducing their contribution to output. As the rewards for rent-seeking rose, this began to affect occupational choice. People sought, and trained for, careers as lobbyists rather than as engineers. Indeed, lobbying, politics and bureaucracy were not the only occupations well rewarded by India's development strategy. The opportunities it created for corruption also implied a strong incentive for concealment of corruption. It resulted in legislation and regulations so Byzantine that firms and governments needed armies of lawyers and accountants, whether to enforce the law or to evade it. In the words of Mancur Olson, 'the direction of social evolution changed': a productive society became a primarily redistributive one. The redistribution, moreover, was not egalitarian: it was biased in favour of those who could mount the maximum lobbying effort.

Indian policy shared these characteristics with other regimes in which government discretion loomed large. However, it also had distinctive features of its own. It involved the creation of a large urban bureaucratic, military, educational and professional salariat; a heavily protected domestic capitalist class and an organized labour class that manned the heavy industry that government patronized, funded and largely owned. It also required a large farmer class that, especially after the Green Revolution, fed the industrialization effort. Each of these constituted a powerful interest group that sought to skew policy in its own favour.

These four classes together dominated policy-making in India's strongly interventionist state. They enjoyed astronomical subsidies on exports, food procurement, fertilizers, irrigation and power, transport rates, education and the public distribution of food to urban consumers. Capital and organized labour in industry were sheltered by an average protective tariff rate of 117% (the highest in the world) and a formidable battery of quantitative import controls. Government employment mushroomed, public enterprises sprouted endlessly and the explosive growth of the army, the bureaucracy and the university establishment created a high-wage, low-productivity island within the economy for the urban middle class. In this lotus-land of government employment, Parkinson's Law prevailed, and the average wage was nine times that in the rest of the economy. Each of the organized groups resisted taxation with a fair degree of success: farm income was totally tax free, and special interest groups could always carve out loopholes and exemptions for themselves. Finally, labour laws guaranteed total job security in the organized sector, and, consequently, productivity lagged behind wages, particularly in the public sector.

These class-based groups reflected the pattern of government policy. Superimposed on this structure of group interests, however, was another inherited from the past, one that reflected the deep divisions of perhaps the most heterogeneous society on the planet, a museum of the species with an infinite variety of races, tribes, castes, languages, religions and cultures. The outcome: a confused multiplicity of group interests and loyalties, 'a functioning anarchy', no doubt, in the famous words of Kenneth Galbraith, but hardly one that functioned too well. The locations of industries, universities, government offices and so on were determined by regional pulls and pressures rather than by functional efficiency. Politically influential groups secured preferential employment for their members through formal quotas and through political and union pressure on the employers. Likewise, the allocation of licences was distorted. Further, since most decisions were not taken by individuals or by small homogeneous groups but were the products of bargaining among a huge variety of organized interests, the entire decision-making process worked in slow motion. Delays in decision-making slowed down adaptation to change and innovation, thus retarding economic growth.

The Indian state had all the standard characteristics graphically described by Olson in his classic, *The Logic of Collective Action*. There was the asymmetry in the distribution of benefits between the organized and the unorganizable: between producers and consumers, between unionized labour and the landless rural work force, between concentrated large-scale industry and small business. There was the consolidation of monopoly through entry barriers erected by organized groups. There was the retardation of innovation as competitive pressures were diluted, as resources were diverted from research into rent-seeking and as vested interests succeeded in aborting change. There were delays in decision-making. There was the Byzantine character of regulation reflecting the play of sectional pressures and counter-pressures and the need to draw a veil of unintelligibility over the sectional purposes that regulation serves. Even the administration and policing of regulation by the government and compliance and evasion by firms became inordinately expensive.

All this led through many tangled paths to a common result – low and stagnant productivity. There were at least eight distinct routes to this unfortunate outcome:

1   The neglect of static comparative advantage in an ISI regime.
2   The exclusion of foreign and domestic competition.
3   The manipulation of industrial location.
4   Appointments based on non-merit considerations.
5   The diversion of resources into rent-seeking.
6   The delays in decision-making.
7   The elimination, on account of labour laws, of the threat of dismissal as a worker-disciplining device.
8   The belief that employment alone and not productivity is socially valuable, with its consequences on the morale of workers and supervisors.

Inefficiency was concentrated in, but not confined to, the public sector. The incompetence of the public sector had a twofold result. It hampered the supply of infrastructural inputs – coal, steel, electricity, railway transport and so on to the rest of the economy and retarded output growth everywhere. It also ensured large losses in most public enterprises, which became in consequence a drain on the exchequer.

The operational inefficiency of public enterprises represented only one part of the problems of the public sector. The other part was its high capital cost. This reflected the capital-intensive character of many of the investments mandated by ISI. It also reflected massive cost inflation through corruption and cost escalation due to the dilatoriness of government decision-making.

The lavish scale of subsidies, the proliferation of public employment, the losses of public enterprises and the high cost of public investment added up to an enormous strain on budgetary resources. Revenues, however, were limited both by resistance to taxation and by the low level and slow growth of output. The initial impact of this was on public investment, which was severely compressed in the late sixties and early seventies. The consequent running down of infrastructure intensified its chronic inefficiency and precipitated a whole series of interrelated crises in steel, cement, energy and transport, the consequence of which was a decade or more of industrial stagnation from the mid-sixties. This came at a time when the problems of the early years of development appeared to be abating: the Green Revolution had eased food shortages, the savings rate had shot up to respectability from its humble origins and even the scarcity of foreign exchange seemed near resolution, thanks to the inflow of remittances. The myth of 'the Hindu rate of growth', a religiously prescribed maximum of 3.5% gained currency.

In the late seventies, this situation compelled a revival of public investment, in particular a restoration of infrastructure. However, revenues remained inelastic, and government consumption rose inexorably. Thus, budget deficits became endemic. The total expenditure of the state and central governments rose to a peak of 32.5% of GDP in 1986–1988, and the net fiscal deficit mounted to 12.5% of GDP. Public

88 Full circle

impecuniosity contrasted strangely with the private frugality implied by a 22 to 24% rate of private saving.

Deficit budgets implied a mounting public debt and rising interest rates as the government competed with and crowded out private borrowers. Servicing costs thus rose more than proportionally to borrowing, further swelling the deficit in a vicious cycle.

The excess demand generated by government deficits was absorbed in part by the restraint on private spending due to higher interest rates. In part, however, it overflowed abroad in large trade deficits. Throughout the seventies, the resulting pressure on foreign exchange reserves was eased by remittances from Indian emigrants – particularly from migrant workers in the Middle East in the wake of the oil boom. In the eighties, however, things changed. The growth of the deficit necessitated artificial stimulation of the inflow of remittances. Large-scale foreign borrowing began, especially from non-resident Indians attracted by exceptionally favourable terms on bank deposits in foreign currency. The rate of growth accelerated quite sharply to 5.5%, a rate sustained throughout the decade by debt-financed investment in infrastructure on the one hand and the creeping liberalization of the eighties on the other. The price for this was the accumulation of high-interest debt. The debt-service ratio as a proportion of current foreign exchange receipts shot up from 9.1% in 1980–81 to 29.7% in 1989–1990.

By the end of the eighties, the mountain of debt was large enough to shake international confidence in India's ability to repay. Political instability, the fiscal irresponsibility of the short-lived governments that accompanied it and finally the Gulf War, which imposed the cost of repatriating hundreds of thousands of Indian workers from the Gulf while depriving India of their foreign exchange earnings, precipitated a crisis which in 1991 drove India into the arms of the International Monetary Fund and willy-nilly down the road to reform.

The decline of the West

While East and South Asia flourished under the new international division of labour, the advanced West and Japan represent the other side of the coin. In the latter, while profit rates have risen, the demand for labour has stagnated or contracted. These consequences have been intensified in recent decades by the Vernon effect: the migration of traditional capital-intensive industry with standardized technology to low-wage regions has left the advanced West with only one source of comparative advantage – high-tech, research-intensive industry. And new technology is a product that – despite WTO and patent legislation – cannot readily be turned into private property. This is a fact at the heart of the West's insistence on strong intellectual property rights legislation and its rigorous enforcement. However, even the strongest patent regimes can rarely safeguard technological secrets for any length of time. And, as explained in Chapter 2, the returns to the innovator are therefore rarely sufficient to offset the many risks and costs that he must incur – the risk of losing out in winner-take-all tournament-type patent races, the sheer uncertainty of research, the difficulty of accurately monitoring the research input of the individual employee, the lack of insurance markets for research and of capital markets to finance it. Private R and D is a precarious venture, and while it may still attract the adventurer, the average rate of return is far from what prudent investors may wish for.

The characteristics of the product and the process of innovation discourage private investment in it. But this is further accentuated by the human capital requirements of a research-based economy. Given the volatility of investment in R and D, the market for researchers is highly unstable and does not encourage people to undertake the long, arduous and expensive process of higher education that would qualify them for research jobs. This in turn adds to the problems of the investor in high technology.

In the effort to exploit the full potential of its comparative advantage in high technology, the advanced West has resorted to two main devices. The first is the technology consortium. High-tech firms have sought to reduce the intensity of competition between them by agreements dividing up the planned field of research between themselves, assigning specific subfields to specific firms and sharing the knowledge generated collectively. This is a path thorny with moral hazard problems but one that does minimize the wasteful duplication of effort involved in patent races.

Most often, however, high tech requires and receives state subsidies. The fig leaf behind which these subsidies are modestly concealed most often is that of military research, easily saleable to the voting public as expenditure essential for defence of the realm. The role of the US Department of Defence in particular in supporting the development of US R and D is immeasurable. There are, of course, limits to the extent to which the electorate will support research expenditure, even if disguised as basic to defence.

There is also, of course, the problem of adapting the composition of the labour force to the requirements of a research economy. This implies a high level of college education, including graduate education, which in turn is possible only if the wage differential between those who have completed college and those who have not is large enough to offset the very high cost in terms of time and money. But for decades now, migration restrictions have protected a high level of unskilled wages in the West. If a high skill premium is added to this, research manpower would become so expensive as to make most R and D unprofitable at world prices for its products. An option is the import of research manpower. These workers would have to be trained in institutions in the advanced West, but those from low-wage economies would have a low opportunity cost of training and would therefore need less of a skill premium than Western workers, and, since their option anyway is low-wage work in their own countries, they will be available to Western employers at substantially lower cost than Western researchers. Thus, the West can partially realize its comparative advantage in R and D through high-tech industries manned largely by high-skilled immigrants.

This does not, however, resolve the long-term dilemma of Western labour in a globalized world. It does not only have to contend with the erosion of the markets

90 Full circle

for its products by low-wage producers in poorer countries and with the counter-attraction of low-wage economies for employers who could potentially have created jobs for it at home. There is also the fact that the lure of Western wages and working conditions has attracted a horde of potential migrants hammering at the gates of entry into the advanced world. Together with the pressure of Western employers eyeing a rich source of cheap labour, this has led to occasional liberalization of immigration. Even when it has not, the common interest of potential employers and employees has led to a flouting of the letter of the law and a substantial inflow of illegal immigrants. Confronted by competition from all these different directions, the Western working class now faces a Hobson's choice. It can either accept massive wage-cuts that would make Western industry competitive with that in lower-wage economies or endure large-scale, long-term unemployment. This is a choice between alternative modes of execution that is unlikely to delight the victim – and, indeed, the victim has resisted vigorously. Throughout the twenty-first century, the discontent of large segments of most Western populations with their economic predicament has been palpable and profound. The discontent has been deepest among those least capable of adapting to the sudden dislocations induced by globalization: the old, the less educated, the worker who has spent a lifetime toiling in a traditional industry who suddenly finds that his industry has vanished and his hard-earned skills have become obsolete. The young college graduate has not shared the same plight. The outcome: sharp cleavages within the population along the lines of the generation gap and the education gap.

Western societies are now more deeply divided than ever before. The plight of older, less educated workers in traditional industry has undermined the pre-existing liberal consensus in favour of open economies, free trade and close economic relationships with other countries. In most advanced economies, it has precipitated a retreat, if not yet a headlong flight, from the world into a protective cocoon of restrictions on trade, immigration and capital outflow. The emotional counterpart and ideological rationale of this retreat is provided by a resurgence of nationalism: a distrust of foreign producers who undercut our own by using 'sweated labour' in their homelands or immigrants who steal away our jobs by working for low wages under exacting conditions on our own soil, a cultural demonization of the foreigner with his strange customs, languages and beliefs which, we would like to claim, alienate him from us beyond all possibility of reconciliation.

Wherever the nationalist isolationist view has controlled policy, as in the United States since 2016, it has led to efforts to insulate the domestic economy, and in particular the older industries, from foreign competition. The outsourcing of labour-intensive operations and the transfer of manufacturing facilities to low-wage economies have been strongly discouraged. One consequence has, indeed, been an increase in demand for labour and consequently in employment and wages. Another, however, has been a fall in the rate of profit and therefore in the incentive to invest. Donald Trump has sought to compensate capitalists by sharp reductions in corporate and personal taxes at the higher end of the spectrum. The tax cut in turn implies a spiralling budget deficit which furnishes the excuse and justification for a drastic contraction in the output of public goods. Electoral resistance to elements of the latter (such as reduction in expenditure on social welfare, health and education) has forced the government to seek other avenues of retrenchment. It has sought to cut back its commitments abroad such as foreign aid and military expenditures that appear at least partly to shore up allies. The United States is in attempted retreat from its earlier role as watchdog of the world to the safety of Fortress America – a safety that has become increasingly illusory as the technology of war itself has been globalized. The United States today is well within the reach of the nuclear-tipped ICBMs of its major, even, indeed, its minor, adversaries and is desperately dependent on early warning systems located in its bases abroad. Another policy outcome of this view is major environmental deregulation, reducing the consumption of public goods like clean water and an unpolluted atmosphere while creating a space for employment-generating but polluting industries like the extraction and use of shale oil and coal and the mining of heavy metals. All of these are measures of short-run relief that invite long-run disaster. Protectionism results in loss of comparative advantage, driving up prices for domestic consumers and undermining markets for exporters as other countries retaliate. Withdrawal from foreign commitments reduces the US sphere of influence and consequently its ability to defend its economic, political and security interests. Environmental deregulation results in job growth today while poisoning the environment not only for posterity but also for the present generation as it ages.

If, despite all these efforts to divert expenditure from public to private goods, demand continues to outstrip output, the budget deficit will be reflected in a trade deficit. And this would have to be financed by an inflow of capital from the outside world. Ever-increasing fractions of the advanced economy would be owned by or indebted to foreigners. As the mountain of debt mounts, it undermines confidence in the ability of the economy to repay, and economic collapse becomes inevitable.

Not that the entire Western world is destined to play out all the phases of this doomsday scenario. Even in the United States, which approximates this model most closely, current presidential policy corresponds only to the views of a clear minority of the electorate, imposed on the majority only through the eccentricities of the US electoral system. However, the upsurge of nationalist ideologies, and in particular the strong aversion to immigration and to immigrants, is a political fact that the West will have to contend with for the foreseeable future.

Demography and the decline of the advanced world

Immigration is, of course, sustained primarily by the wage differentials between the West and the rest, and the long-run factors we have listed previously that drive globalization are tending to narrow these differences. There is, however, another long-run factor that works in the opposite direction. This is demography. Throughout the West, as well as on the fast-developing Pacific rim of Asia, the market has penetrated deeply into the structure and functioning of the nuclear family. Women in these economies are no longer confined to 'domestic bliss' within the charmed circle of the family; they work in increasing numbers in the outside labour market. And as their wages and employment opportunities have risen, so has the opportunity cost of the enormously time-consuming business of child-bearing and rearing. Birth rates in these societies have collapsed, just as they did during the earlier phase of the dissolution of the extended family and its replacement by the nuclear family. So dramatic, indeed, has the collapse been that total fertility (the number of children born to the average woman during her entire reproductive life span) has fallen below the replacement rate of 2.1% in almost all of North America, Europe and East Asia. According to World Bank data in 2016, Canada is emptying out again, with a total fertility rate of 1.6. US fertility is well below replacement despite being buoyed up by a high rate among immigrant Latinos. Populations are in decline all over Europe, with the South European nations of Portugal, Spain, Italy and Greece hurtling towards extinction with fertility rates near 1.3. Even more drastic is the demographic predicament of East Asia, with the Four Tigers averaging 1.2, Japan at 1.4 and China at 1.6. All these populations face the problems not only of numerical decline but of rapid aging as well. They are hurtling towards a future in which a vast and multiplying horde of retirees must be supported by an ever-diminishing work force.

Africa, in sharp contrast, is extraordinarily prolific. Barring Afghanistan and the island republic of East Timor, every country that figures among the top 30 in the ranking of sovereign states by total fertility is African, with Niger soaring above 7 and Angola, Chad, Mali, the Democratic Republic of Congo and Somalia not far below. In many of these countries, mortality does indeed take a heavy toll. Yet there can be little doubt that if these rates persist, the racial composition of the world will change rapidly. Further, the demographics tend to widen wage differentials between the advanced West and poverty-stricken parts of Africa, Latin America and the Middle East and spur migratory pressures from the latter to the former. Japan, Korea, Taiwan and perhaps even China may face similar immigration pressures in the long run, though temporarily shielded today by their linguistic and cultural distinctiveness. East Asia and the advanced West could of course absorb these immigrants and use them to resolve the labour shortages they will inevitably face – the shortage of the cheap and willing labour that could restore the competitiveness of their manufactures and the shortage of the younger workers who could support their aging pensioners. But large-scale immigration is a certain recipe for hostile, xenophobic and possibly violent resistance by the host population.

Outsiders: the beneficiaries and the losers

The Industrial Revolution of nineteenth-century Europe induced economic growth elsewhere in the world. As David Ricardo saw it, it led to pressures on Europe's natural resource base, to scarcities and rising prices of natural resources that stimulated the exploitation of emptier lands outside Western Europe, notably in the New World. In particular, it propelled the economic development of North America initially through the expansion of its primary exports. The contemporary industrialization of densely populated Asia has had similar effects elsewhere, mainly in the thinly populated, as-yet-little-exploited interiors of large landmasses. The most notable outsider to have benefited thus from the Asian Miracle has been Australia, the only advanced economy to have escaped a technical recession (two consecutive quarters of GDP contraction) in decades. Thanks to proximity and its low man-land ratio, Australia has played for East and South Asia the role that the United States did for Western Europe in the nineteenth century. Its empty internal frontier in West Australia and the Northern Territory has supplied Asia's multiplying need for metals (iron ore, gold, copper and aluminium) in addition to coal and the traditional Australian exports of wheat, wool and beef from Queensland and the South Eastern states. A similar beneficiary of Asian growth, though slightly handicapped by distance, is Brazil. From its vast interior, Brazil caters to Asian demand for agricultural products like oilseeds, sugar, animal fodder, poultry and beef, as well as fuel and minerals like oil and iron ore. A third beneficiary is South Africa, which exports precious metals and minerals (gold, platinum and diamonds), mineral fuels (coal and petroleum products), iron and manganese ores and alloys, aluminium and agricultural produce like fruit and nuts. In all three countries, primary exports have led to infrastructure development and urbanization. In Brazil and South Africa, where wages are still low relative to the advanced West and the Asian pioneers, infrastructural and urban expansion has enabled industrialization, including exports of vehicles, machinery and computers. Australian growth and urbanization have supported the development and export of financial and educational services catering to the Asian, as well as the domestic, market.

Other beneficiaries of Asian growth and of the worldwide expansion of demand it induced are African and Latin American countries, which have enjoyed soaring markets for their primary products in consequence – countries like Ethiopia (coffee, oilseeds and dried legumes, gold, sheep and goat meat, hides and leather) and Ivory Coast (cocoa, rubber, oil, fruits and nuts, gold). The low levels of African wages have prompted predictions of labour-intensive industrialization *à la* Asia. In particular, the substantial output of raw cotton in East Africa has fuelled expectations of a rapid growth of a textile and apparel industry. These have been largely belied, partly because of the counterattraction of the primary sector for investors – the so-called 'Dutch disease' – and partly because of the complete domination of the domestic clothing market by imports of second-hand clothing from the West. In Ethiopia, for example, textiles and garments have developed, but slowly, despite prolonged and massive government encouragement. On the other hand, the entirely unexpected and explosive growth of floriculture for export has within a few short years catapulted the country into the ranks of the world's major suppliers of roses, other cut flowers and trees alongside the traditional giants, the Netherlands, Ecuador, Colombia and Kenya. This has been a response to the new logistics of instant electronic communication and rapid air transport, which have enabled Ethiopia to exploit the geographical advantages of her climate and location (relative to the world's main flower auction centre at Aalsmeer near Amsterdam airport), as well as her abundant low-wage labour. Generally, however, economic development through export of

94 Full circle

natural resource products is subject to two major limitations. First, it is often highly unstable due to the volatility of international commodity prices. Second, its main beneficiaries are the owners of the natural resources, who are often too few in number to constitute a significant market for domestic manufactures; even where the state is the owner, the consequences of an expansion in demand for the resource depend on the balance of power within the state: it could well be private enrichment of a political elite rather than broad-based growth and has been so in the 'kleptocracies' that figure prominently in the horror stories of the recent economic development of resource-rich regions.

Conclusion

The changes over the last half-century or so in the technology of transport, communications, management and production and the associated changes in the structure of demand and the distribution of world income have made low labour cost a decisive advantage in production. Unlike in earlier years, it may now outweigh the advantage of economies of scale (which meanwhile have probably diminished in importance) in very many industries. Had labour been perfectly mobile internationally, this would have made no difference to the relative economic performance of different countries since labour costs would have been uniform everywhere. However, it is not. Labour immobility is in part a consequence of the physical cost of moving labour. More importantly, it is the outcome of the immigration restrictions of sovereign states seeking to protect the high wage levels of domestic workers. Given the reach and power of modern states, these restrictions are a pervasive fact of modern life and define labour endowment as a fixed characteristic of any country, one that it inherits from its history and can change only in the long run through natural population growth or decline.

Economies that have been successful over long periods of time accumulate large populations that, in the absence of Malthusian catastrophes, maintain themselves even after their days of success are over. Their dense populations imply low labour costs. This would have been a significant economic asset, a crucial element of comparative advantage, if labour costs were central to the technology that currently dominated the world economy. We have argued that, for two centuries since the Industrial Revolution, this was not so. Scale economies were a far more important factor, and they worked against poor, densely populated countries. By the late eighteenth century, densely populated Asia was, for reasons explained in Chapter 3, lagging well behind Western Europe. The 200 years that followed widened this gap into a Great Divergence.

From the 1960s, the picture changed. The technological transformation of the late twentieth century integrated for the first time the labour surpluses of Asia into the mainstream of world trade and dramatically accelerated Asian growth. What was earlier a liability now became a major asset. The wage differentials that the advanced West had sought sedulously to safeguard through migration restrictions became the principal source of Asian catch-up and Western stagnation. Such are the ironies of history.

Notes

1 The section on 'The Sequencing of the Miracle: China's short and India's long lag' contains extracts originally published in *Planning and Economic Policy in India*, Copyright 1996 ©Manabendu Chattopadhyay, Pradeep Maiti, Mihir Rakshit, All rights reserved. Reproduced with the permission of the copyright holders and the publishers, SAGE Publications India Pvt. Ltd, New Delhi.

2 A. Young, The Tyranny of Numbers: Confronting the Statistical Realities of the East Asian Growth Experience, *The Quarterly Journal of Economics*, 110 (1995), pp. 641–680.

3 L. Lau, J. Il Kim, The Sources of Economic Growth in the Newly Industrialized Countries on the Pacific Rim, in L. R. Klein, C.-T. Yu (eds.), *The Economic Development of ROC and the Pacific Rim in the 1990s and Beyond*, 1994.

4 P. Krugman, The Myth of Asia's Miracle, *Foreign Affairs*, 1994.

5 B. Ohlin, *International and Interregional Trade*, Cambridge, MA: Harvard University Press, 1933.

6 P. A. Samuelson, International Trade and the Equalization of Factor Prices, *Economic Journal*, 58 (230), 1948, pp. 163–184.

7 Note that the predictions of the neo-classical theory of trade – of higher rates of profit in poorer countries and consequent large flows of capital from rich to poor countries – are precisely echoed by Lenin's theory of imperialism. The common conclusions of both were falsified by the realities of international investment before 1965. Of course, the two models differed very widely in their interpretation of the consequences for the welfare of the poor countries.

8 T. M. Rybczynski, Factor Endowment and Relative Commodity Prices, *Economica*, 22 (88), 1955, pp. 336–341.

9 K. Akamatsu, A Historical Pattern of Economic Growth in Developing Countries, *Journal of Developing Economies*, 1 (s1), 1962, pp. 3–25.

10 R. Vernon, L. T. Wells, International Trade and International Investment in the Product Life Cycle, *Quarterly Journal of Economics*, 80 (2), 1966, pp. 190–207.

EPILOGUE

We are at the end of our journey through time. But the relentless march of technology into the unknown future continues at an ever-accelerating pace, and the reader may well expect, if not crystal ball-gazing, at least some random speculations about what the coming decades may bring. In particular, one may well ask whether technological progress has already spelled the end of geography – much as Francis Fukuyama announced some decades ago – and perhaps prematurely – 'the end of history'.[1] Unlike open-ocean navigation or coal-and-iron technology or the railways or the internal combustion engine, information technology and its offshoots are not tied to specific geographical features or resource endowments. Can we infer, therefore, that it will not confer a special advantage or impose a special cost on any particular region or country? Will technological progress be geographically neutral in its impact?

As we have seen in the previous chapter, over the last half-century, innovations in transport and, especially, in communications have virtually annihilated distance as an economic consideration. Geography, however, continues to matter. Certain resources – climate, topography and geology, for instance – are immutable characteristics of certain locations and cannot be transported elsewhere. Moreover, man-made restrictions artificially impede the flow of other resources (and goods) across national boundaries. In particular, migration restrictions hinder the free flow of labour and tend thereby to perpetuate international wage differentials and income inequalities. It was the new technology of transport and communication and the innovations in production which it induced that enabled the world to adjust to these man-made restrictions and powered the surge of Asian growth over the last fifty years.

Indeed, since the mid-1960s, there has been a remarkable convergence in factor prices and per capita incomes, at least between Asia and the West. However, except for a couple of Asian Tigers, this process of factor price equalization is still far from

Epilogue **97**

complete. Are the current trends in technology likely to widen the price differentials that remain? Could international trade offset this divergence and restore the pressure for equalization of prices and per capita incomes?

We lack the expertise to predict the future of technology, but, according to many, the future lies in robotics and artificial intelligence. If so, labour–abundant low–wage economies face dark days again. If firms in high–wage economies can robotize their labour–intensive operations, they can so increase the productivity of their labour that the attraction of low–wage locations will disappear; so will the profitability of export of labour–intensive manufactures from Asia and other low–wage countries. In essence, we will witness a reenactment on a magnified global scale of the early nineteenth–century scenario of the mechanization of cotton spinning and weaving in the British Industrial Revolution, the process that destroyed the cost advantage that Indian textiles had enjoyed earlier in the world market on account of low wages. The catastrophic consequences of this for the Indian economy have been sketched in Chapter 3. A repetition of these outcomes in the near future could spell disaster for the low–wage world. Asian economies like Korea which have already graduated to higher wage levels and robotized significant sectors of their economies would hardly be affected. But India, for one, would pay heavily for its thirty–year lag behind the pioneers of the Asian Miracle.

It is important to recognize at this point that while the induction of robots might enable the advanced West to reclaim many of the industries it had earlier surrendered to Asia, it will not add to the demand for labour in the West. Robots do not create jobs anywhere. Indeed, in the United States and Western Europe, they may spark a neo–Luddite uprising that could conceivably arrest, or at least delay, the onset of large–scale robotization. However, such a reprieve may only be temporary. Given the demographics of the advanced world, the prospective decline in its numbers and the even faster decline in its working population as it ages, labour surpluses and consequent resistance to robotics may not be long–term phenomena, especially if the advanced economies have meanwhile shut their doors to the inflow of immigrants from poorer countries (as, indeed, they appear likely to do).

There are, however, aspects of work that lend themselves well to robotization and others that do not. Mechanical repetitive operations can readily be delegated to robots, while jobs that call for adaptations to new non–programmable situations cannot. Production takes place not in hermetically sealed labs but in often–uncontrollable environments and in the context of unpredictable business situations. It is difficult, if not impossible, to design robots that could respond appropriately to such changes in circumstance. Mass production processes, assembly–line operations and the like can be easily automated. On the other hand, customization, uniqueness and exclusiveness are far more difficult to achieve with robot operators, in part because it would be much too expensive to design robots for small–scale or one–time use.

A similar duality exists in the realm of services. Bank tellers have been largely replaced by robots. Call centres, medical transcription and delivery services can all

98 Epilogue

be easily robotized. Robots have even begun reading the news on TV (though one wonders what their television rating points are like). Work that calls for emotional qualities — empathy, sensitivity and the like — is a different matter altogether. An automaton cannot be a fully satisfactory nurse, childcare-giver, geriatric social worker or psychotherapist. Or, for that matter, a teacher.

Most of the operations that have migrated to the low-wage economies in the last few decades are of the mechanical, repetitive variety and can therefore be readily robotized, opening up the possibility of their return to the advanced world. If they are to adjust to such a future, the poorer countries need to change the composition of their labour forces, to train larger numbers of their workers in skills that could resist robotization. These include traditional handicraft skills which will need extensive marketing efforts, but given the vast diversity of handicraft traditions worldwide, it is doubtful whether any country can ever carve out anything more than a small niche market for its handicrafts. Personalized services offer a more promising field. As the advanced world ages and as the demands of its labour market on families with young children become more insistent, its demand for nursing or care of children and seniors will mushroom. Shortages of nurses and school teachers have already become ubiquitous in the West, inducing substantial migration of nurses from their traditional supply bases like Kerala — though nothing similar has yet occurred among school-teachers.

The problem with personalized services, of course, is that they cannot be supplied through remote access. (If they could, they could probably also have been robotized.) They require the supplier to migrate to his clientele. And this means prying open the door of migration barriers that most advanced countries are in the process of reinforcing. Perhaps the felt needs for certain kinds of services may lead to exemptions for specific skills. But a generalized hostility towards immigration would be something that the migrant would still have to cope with. In any event, a boom in the demand for personalized services by immigrant labour is unlikely to compensate for a collapse in the market for manufacturing labour. Labour, especially unskilled labour, and countries burdened with a surplus of it are doomed to a bleak future if an Invasion of the Bots is at hand.

Things could get even worse if meanwhile artificial intelligence develops effective machines that could learn on the job. Robots would then pose a threat not only to unskilled, repetitive jobs but to skilled work as well.[2] We would then face a truly jobless future. This, of course, would spell the end of the world as we have known it, of the world of effort and incentive, and perhaps the beginning of an age of boundless leisure. Robots would still have to be designed and owned, but their output would have to be equitably distributed if a peaceful transition to such an age is to be ensured. Otherwise, of course, we could all be consumed in an apocalyptic conflict between jobless peoples and classes and the owning elite. But before we are tempted into even wilder flights of fancy, let us abandon our speculations and return to the more mundane solidity of the past and the present, to the tangible facts that we have tried in this book to understand. The future, after all, is unknowable as well as unknown.

Notes

1 F. Fukuyama, *The End of History and the Last Man*, New York: Free Press, 1992.
2 We do not go into the other great risk that the development of AI has created, the risk so brilliantly highlighted by Yuval Noah Harari (*Homo Deus,* Penguin-Random House, UK, 2015). This is the danger that AI will enable machines to explore and get to know our values and preferences even better, perhaps, than we know them ourselves. This will enable corporate and government entities who control these machines to manipulate our preferences and mould our economic and political choices. We will then have lost our sovereignty and entered a world where free will is an illusion and an anachronism.

REFERENCES

Acemoglu, D., S. Johnson, J. Robinson, The Colonial Origins of Comparative Economic Development, *American Economic Review*, 91, 2001, pp. 1369–1401.

Acemoglu, D., S. Johnson, J. Robinson, Institutions as a Fundamental Cause of Long-Run Economic Development, in *Handbook of Economic Growth*, 2005.

Acemoglu, D., S. Johnson, J. Robinson, Reversal of Fortune: Geography and Institutions in the Making of the Modern World Income Distribution, *The Quarterly Journal of Economics*, 117 (4), 2002, pp. 1231–1294.

Acemoglu, D., S. Johnson, J. Robinson, The Rise of Europe: Atlantic Trade, Institutional Change and Economic Growth, *American Economic Review*, 95 (3), 2005, pp. 546–579.

Akamatsu, K., A Historical Pattern of Economic Growth in Developing Countries, *Journal of Developing Economies*, 1 (s1), 1962, pp. 3–25.

Allen, R. C., India in the Great Divergence, in T. J. Hatton, K. H. O'Rourke, A. M. Taylor (eds.), *The New Comparative Economic History: Essays in Honor of Jeffery G. Williamson*, Cambridge, MA: MIT Press, 2007, pp. 9–32.

Allen, R. C., Technology and the Great Divergence: Global Economic Inequality since 1820, *Explorations in Economic History*, 49, 2012, pp. 1–16.

Allen, R. C., T. E. Murphy, E. B. Schneider, The Colonial Origins of the Great Divergence, a Labour Market Approach, *Journal of Economic History*, 72 (4), 2012, pp. 863–894.

Anderson, J., E. van Wincoop, Trade Costs, *Journal of Economic Literature*, 42, 2004, pp. 691–751.

Baldwin, R. E., Patterns of Development in Newly Settled Regions, *Manchester School of Economic and Social Studies*, 24 (2), 1956, pp. 161–179.

Baumol, W. J., *The Free Market Innovation Machine*, Princeton: Princeton University Press, 2002.

Behrens, K., C. Gaigne, G. I. P. Ottaviano, J. F. Thisse, Is Remoteness a Locational Disadvantage? *Journal of Economic Geography*, 6 (3), 2006, pp. 347–368.

Boserup, E., *The Conditions of Agricultural Growth*, London: Allen and Unwin, 1965.

Broadberry, S., B. Gupta, The Early Modern Great Divergence: Wages, Prices and Economic Development in Europe and Asia, 1500–1800, *Economic History Review*, 59 (1), 2006, pp. 2–31.

References **101**

Broadberry, S., et al., *British Economic Growth 1270–1870*, Cambridge: Cambridge University Press, 2015.

Capra, F., *Learning from Leonardo*, 2013.

Chaudhuri, K. N., *The Trading World of Asia and the English East India Company, 1660–1760*, Cambridge: Cambridge University Press, 2006.

Cipolla, C., *Guns, Sails and Empires*, New York: Minerva, 1965.

Clark, G., K. H. O'Rourke, A. M. Taylor, The Growing Dependence of Britain on Trade during the Industrial Revolution, *The Scandinavian Economic History Review*, 62 (2), 2014, pp. 109–136.

Clingingsmith, D., J. G. Williamson, Deindustrialization in Eighteenth and Nineteenth Century India, *Explorations in Economic History*, 45 (3), 2008, pp. 209–234.

Crafts, N. F. R., British Economic Growth, 1760–1831, *Economic History Review*, IInd series, 36 (2), 1983, pp. 177–199.

Crafts, N. F. R., *British Economic Growth during the Industrial Revolution*, Oxford: Clarendon Press, 1985.

Crafts, N. F. R., C. K. Harley, Output Growth and the Industrial Revolution, *Economic History Review*, 45 (4), 1992, pp. 703–730.

Crone, P., *Slaves on Horses: The Evolution of the Islamic Polity*, Cambridge: Cambridge University Press, 1980.

Currey, B., G. Hugo, *Famine as a Geographical Phenomenon*, Boston: GeoJournal Library, 1984.

Dattel, G., The South's Mighty Gamble on King Cotton, *American Heritage Magazine*, 2010.

Deane, P., *The First Industrial Revolution*, Cambridge: Cambridge University Press, 1979.

Diamond, J., *Guns, Germs and Steel: The Fates of Human Societies*, New York and London: W.W. Norton & Company, 1997.

Digby, W., *'Prosperous' British India: A Revelation from Official Records*, London: T. Fisher Unwin, 1901.

Eberhard, W., *A History of China*, Berkeley: University of California Press, 1960.

Eltis, D., The Total Product of Barbados, *Journal of Economic History*, 55, 1995, pp. 321–336.

Engerman, S. L., K. L. Sokoloff, Institutions, Factor Endowments and Paths of Development in the New World, *Journal of Economic Perspectives*, 14 (3), 2000, pp. 217–232.

Fenoaltea, S., Slavery and Supervision in Comparative Perspective: A Model, *Journal of Economic History*, 44 (3), 1984, pp. 635–668.

Fernihough, A., K. H. O'Rourke, *Coal and the European Industrial Revolution*, NBER Working Paper 19802, 2014.

Findlay, R., K. H. O'Rourke, *Power and Plenty: Trade, War and the World Economy in the Second Millennium*, Princeton: Princeton University Press, 2001.

Flynn, D. O., Fiscal Crisis and the Decline of Spain (Castile), *Journal of Economic History*, 42 (1), 1982, pp. 139–147.

Freeman, D. B., *The Straits of Malacca: Gateway or Gauntlet?* Montreal: McGill-Queen's University Press, 2003.

Fukuyama, F., *The End of History and the Last Man*, New York: Free Press, 1992.

Gallup, J., J. Sachs, A. Mellinger, Geography and Economic Development, *International Regional Science Review*, 22, 1999, pp. 179–232.

Gordon, S., The Limited Adoption of European-Style Military Forces by Eighteenth Century Rulers in India, *The Indian Social and Economic History Review*, 35 (3), 1998.

Greif, A., Contract Enforceability and Economic Institutions in Early Trade: The Maghribi Traders' Coalition, *American Economic Review*, 83 (3), 1993, pp. 525–548.

Griliches, Z., D. Jorgenson, The Explanation of Productivity Change, *Review of Economic Studies*, 34 (3), 1967, pp. 249–283.

102 References

Guha, A. S., *An Evolutionary View of Economic Growth*, Oxford: Clarendon Press, 1981.

Guha, A. S., The ISI Model: Its Rationale and Limitations, in M. Chattopadhyay, P. Maiti, M. Rakshit (eds.), *Planning and Economic Policy in India*, New Delhi: Sage Publications India, 1996.

Guha, A. S., B. Guha, Reversal of Fortune Revisited: The Geography of Transport and the Changing Balance of World Economic Power, *Revista di Storia Economica*, 2, 2014, pp. 161–188.

Guha, B., Ancient Wisdom, *The Telegraph*, February 17, 2015.

Guha, B., Who Will Monitor the Monitors; Informal Law Enforcement and Collusion at Champagne, *Journal of Economic Behaviour and Organization*, 83 (2), 2012, pp. 261–277.

Harari, Y. N., *Homo Deus*, London: Penguin Random House, 2015.

Hoffman, P. T., Why Was It Europeans Who Conquered the World? *The Economic History Review*, 72, 2012, pp. 601–633.

Holzman, J., *The Nabobs in England: A Study of the Returned Anglo-Indian, 1760–1785*, New York: Columbia University Press, 1926.

Hourani, G. F., *Arab Seafaring in the Indian Ocean*, Princeton: Princeton University Press, 1995.

Jones, E. L., *The European Miracle: Environments, Economies and Geopolitics in the History of Europe and Asia*, Cambridge: Cambridge University Press, 1981.

Krugman, P., The Myth of Asia's Miracle, *Foreign Affairs*, 1994.

Landes, D. S., *The Unbound Prometheus: Technological Change and Industrial Development in Western Europe from 1750 to the Present*. Cambridge and New York: Press Syndicate of the University of Cambridge, 1969.

Landes, D. S., Why Europe and the West? Why Not China? *Journal of Economic Perspectives*, 20 (2), 2006, pp. 3–22.

Lane, F. C., Pepper Prices Before da Gama, *Journal of Economic History*, 28 (4), 1968, pp. 590–597.

Lane, F. C., Recent Studies on the Economic History of Venice, *Journal of Economic History*, 23 (3), 1963, pp. 312–334.

Lattimore, O., *Inner Asian Frontiers of China*, New York: American Geographical Society, 1940.

Lawrence, L., J. Il Kim, The Sources of Economic Growth in the Newly Industrialized Countries on the Pacific Rim, in L. R. Klein, C.-T. Yu (eds.), *The Economic Development of ROC and the Pacific Rim in the 1990s and Beyond*, 1994.

Levathes, L., *When China Ruled the Seas: The Treasure Fleet of the Dragon Throne*, Oxford: Oxford University Press, 1997.

Leyburn, J. G., On the Shoulders of Giants: A Shandean Postscript by Robert K. Merton, *Social Forces*, 44 (4), 1966, pp. 603–604.

Ma, H., *Ying Yai Sheng Lan (Overall Survey of the Ocean's Shores)*, 1433, J. V. G. Mills (tr. and ed.), London: Cambridge University Press, 1970.

Maddison, A., *Class Structure and Economic Growth: India & Pakistan since the Moghuls*, London: Routledge, 2013.

Maddison, A., *The World Economy*, Paris: Development Centre of the Organisation for Economic Cooperation and Development, 2006.

Mansfield, E., *Industrial Research and Technological Change*, New York: W. W. Norton, 1968.

Mansfield, E., M. Schwartz, S. Wagner, Imitation Costs and Patents: An Empirical Study, *Economic Journal*, 91 (364), 1981, pp. 907–918.

Mathias, P., *The First Industrial Nation: An Economic History of Britain 1700–1914*, London: Routledge, 1969.

McCloskey, D., *Bourgeois Equality: How Ideas, Not Capital or Institutions, Enriched the World*, Chicago: University of Chicago Press, 2016.

References **103**

Menard, R., Transport Costs and Long-Range Trade 1300–1800, in J. Tracy (ed.), *Political Economy of Merchant Empires, 1350–1750*, Cambridge: Cambridge University Press, 1991.

Mokyr, J., *A Culture of Growth: The Origins of the Modern Economy*, Princeton: Princeton University Press, 2016.

Mokyr, J., *Twenty-Five Centuries of Technological Change*, London: Routledge, 2001.

Murton, B., VI.4: Famine, in *The Cambridge World History of Food*, vol. 2, New York: Cambridge University Press.

Needham, J., *Science and Civilization in China*, Cambridge: Cambridge University Press, 2008.

Nef, J. U., The Progress of Technology and the Growth of Large Scale Industry in Great Britain, 1540–1640, *Economic History Review*, 1st series, 5 (1), 1934, pp. 3–24.

Ohlin, B., *International and Interregional Trade*, Cambridge, MA: Harvard University Press, 1933.

O'Rourke, K. H., J. G. Williamson, Did Vasco da Gama Matter for European Markets? *The Economic History Review*, 62, 2009, pp. 655–684.

Parker, G., *The Military Revolution*, Cambridge: Cambridge University Press, 1988.

Parry, J. H., *Discovery of the Sea*, Berkeley: University of California Press, 1981.

Parthasarathi, P., Cotton Textiles in the Indian Subcontinent, 1200–1850, in P. Parthasarathi and G. Riello (eds.), *The Spinning World: A Global History of Cotton Textiles, 1200–1850*, Oxford and New York: Oxford University Press, 2011.

Parthasarathi, P., Rethinking Wages and Competitiveness in the Eighteenth Century: Britain and South India, *Past and Present*, 158 (1), 1998, pp. 79–109.

Pomeranz, K. H., *The Great Divergence: China, Europe and the Modern World Economy*, Princeton: Princeton University Press, 2000.

Qaisar, A. J., Shipbuilding in the Mughal Empire in the Seventeenth Century, *Indian Economic and Social History Review*, 5 (2), 1968, pp. 149–170.

Ray, I., Shipbuilding in Bengal under Colonial Rule: A Case of 'DeIndustrialisation', *The Journal of Transport History*, 16 (1), 1995.

Redding, S., A. Venables, Economic Geography and International Inequality, *Journal of International Economics*, 62, 2004, pp. 53–82.

Rei, C., The Organization of Eastern Merchant Empires, *Explorations in Economic History*, 48, 2011, pp. 116–135.

Rossabi, M., *China and Inner Asia from 1368 to the Present Day*, Edmonton: Pica Press, 1975.

Rybczynski, T. M., Factor Endowment and Relative Commodity Prices, *Economica*, 22 (88), 1955, pp. 336–341.

Sachs, J., Government, Geography and Growth, *Foreign Affairs*, September–October 2012.

Samuelson, P. A., International Trade and the Equalization of Factor Prices, *Economic Journal*, 58 (230), 1948, pp. 163–184.

Saunders, J., *The History of the Mongol Conquests*, London: Routledge and Kegan Paul Ltd, 1971.

Scherer, F. M., Firm Size, Market Structure, Opportunity and the Output of Patented Inventions, *American Economic Review*, 55 (5), 1965, pp. 1097–1125.

Schmookler, J., *Invention and Economic Growth*, Cambridge, MA: Harvard University Press, 1960.

Sen, A., *Poverty and Famines: An Essay on Entitlements and Deprivation*, Oxford: Oxford University Press, 1983.

Sheridan, R. B., The Wealth of Jamaica in the Eighteenth Century, *Journal of Economic History*, 18 (2), 1965, pp. 292–311.

Solow, R. M., Technical Change and the Aggregate Production Function, *Review of Economics and Statistics*, 39 (3), 1957, pp. 312–320.

Stephenson, C., *Medieval Feudalism*, Ithaca: Cornell University Press, 1942.

104 References

Thomas, B., *The Industrial Revolution and the Atlantic Economy*, London: Routledge, 1993.

Unger, R. W. (ed.), *Shipping and Economic Growth, 1350–1850*, New York: Brill, 2011.

Vernon, R., L. T. Wells, International Trade and International Investment in the Product Life Cycle, *Quarterly Journal of Economics*, 80 (2), 1966, pp. 190–207.

Vries, de J., A. van der Woude, *The First Modern Economy: Success, Failure, and Perseverance of the Dutch Economy, 1500–1815*, Cambridge: Cambridge University Press, 1997.

Waley-Cohen, J., China and Western Technology in the Late Eighteenth Century, *The American Historical Review*, 98 (5), 1993, pp. 1525–1544.

Waters, D. W., *The Art of Navigation in England in Elizabethan and Early Stuart Times*, London: Hollis and Carter, 1958.

Waters, D. W., Cloth Production and International Competition in the Seventeenth Century, *Economic History Review*, 13 (2), 1960, pp. 209–221.

Waters, D. W., *The Iberian Bases of the English Art of Navigation in the Sixteenth Century*, 1970.

Waters, D. W., Taxation and the Decline of Empires, in C. Wilson (ed.), *Economic History and the Historian*, 1969.

Wilson, C., The Economic Decline of the Netherlands, *Economic History Review*, 9 (2), 1939, pp. 111–159.

Wrigley, E. A., *The Path to Sustained Growth. England's Transition from an Organic Economy to an Industrial Revolution*, Cambridge: Cambridge University Press, 2016.

Wrigley, E. A., R. S. Schofield, *The Population History of England, 1541–1871: A Reconstruction*, Cambridge, MA: Harvard University Press, 1981.

Young, A., The Tyranny of Numbers: Confronting the Statistical Realities of the East Asian Growth Experience, *The Quarterly Journal of Economics*, 110, 1995, pp. 641–680.

INDEX

Acemoglu, D. 3–6, 8, 51, 52, 55
Afghanistan 92
Africa 14; Asian growth and 93; fertility rate 92
Age of Immobility 25–26
Agricultural Revolution 56
agriculture 6, 26, 27, 54, 59, 60; Asia 24, 29–30, 83, 93; British 70; China 27–28, 33, 76, 83; Europe and 29, 30; India 41, 43–45; innovations in 15, 21; nomads and 30; Spain 61; urbanization and 2
AJR (Acemoglu, Johnson and Robinson) 3–6, 8, 51, 52, 55
Allen, R. C. 13, 14, 52–53
American War of Independence 66
Americas 61, 62, 68; economic growth 49–50; Europe s access to 39, 49; geographical differences 52–53; land/man ratio 72; reversal of fortune in 54; Spanish expeditions 7; *see also* Caribbean; Latin America; North America; United States (US)
AMS (Allen, Murphy and Schneider) model 52–53
Antwerp 57, 58, 61, 63
Arrow, Kenneth 14
artificial intelligence 97, 98
Art of Navigation, The (de Medina) 58
Asia/Asian growth (Miracle) 75; agriculture 24, 29–30, 83, 93; beneficiaries of 92–94; continental preoccupations 24; export-led industrialization 81; fall of empires 1; Gang of Four 81; geography 24;

industrialization 81–83; international division of labour 81, 83; land transport 24; newly industrializing countries (NIC) 76, 81; per capita incomes 81; policies of 24; rates of growth 76–77; urbanization 82; wages 81; West s domination 40–45
astronomy 12
Atlantic Europe 1
Aurangzeb 45
Australia 3, 5, 6, 49, 71; Asian growth and 93; natural resources of 39; railway building 44
automaton 98
Avalokeshvara 34
Aztec 49, 50, 61

Baldwin, Robert 51, 52, 53
Bank of England 60
Barbados 50–51, 55
battle of Lepanto 61
Bell, Alexander Graham 11
Bengal famine of 1770 40
Benz, Karl 72
Bessemer, Henry 11
Bessemer process 11
birth rates 92; *see* fertility/fertility rate
Black Death 57, 59
Boserup, Ester 15
Brazil 51, 53, 55, 58, 61; abolition of slavery 52; Asian growth and 93; Madeira model 50; sugar boom 49, 50
Britain: agriculture 70; Bank of England 60; climacteric 71–73; Corn Laws

106 Index

70, 71; Elizabethan era 57, 58; Indian government of 40–45; Industrial Revolution 56–57, 66–70; ocean navigation and warfare technology 56, 57–59; plague 57; population growth 59–60; reversals of fortune 56–57; Statute of Monopolies 60
budget deficits, India 87–88

Cabot, Sebastian 58
Canada 3, 6, 8, 19, 51; fertility rate 92
capital-abundant countries 77, 78
capital-intensive goods 77, 78
care-intensive activities 54
Caribbean 5, 32, 49, 51 52, 53; GDP growth 54 55; Madeira model 50; plantation monocultures 50; slave-driven economies 54 55; Spanish conquest and 61
Certain Errors in Navigation (Wright) 58
China 33–35, 83–84; agriculture 27–28, 33, 76, 83; coal/coalfields 39; dictatorship 83; geopolitics 34; Grand Canal 26, 34; Great Wall 26, 29, 33, 34; imperial system of 39; industrialization 39, 76, 83–84; labour-intensive light industry 84; Mao 84; military security 33; socialist economy 83; Western Europe *vs.* 39
Clark, G. 70
Clive, Robert 40
coke-smelting of iron 13, 20, 66–67
Columbus, Christopher 24, 49, 54
combustion engine 8
Commercial Revolution 6
Compendium of the Art of Navigation (Zamorano) 58
Corn Laws 70, 71
Cortes, Martin 58
cotton gin 50, 68
cotton textiles/textile mills, India 42–43
countries, fixed characteristics 75
Cromwell, Oliver 60
Cuba 50–51

Damascus steel 43
Darby, Abraham 13, 20, 66–67
da Vinci, Leonardo 10
demand, and innovations 14–16
de Medina, Pedro 58
demography 91–92
Deng Xiaoping 83
de Silva, Nuna 58
Diamond, Jared 39
Diesel, Rudolf 72
Drake, Francis 58

Dutch/Dutch Republic 8, 12, 19, 24, 31, 32; Anglo-Dutch struggle 61; as commercial power 56, 57; as economic powerhouse 2; eventual failure of 63–66; maritime trade 36; Spain and 62, 63; Sri Lanka and 37–38
Dutch East India Company (VOC) 65, 68

econometric exercises 3–4
economic growth: institutions as determinants of 5–6; as a linear process 5; regional pattern 7; success-and-failure stories 3
economies of scale 78–81
Edward VI of Britain 57
Engel's Law 79
Engerman, S. L. 51, 52, 53, 54–55
England *see* Britain
ES (Engerman and Sokoloff) model 51, 52, 53, 54–55
Ethiopia, Asian growth and 93
Eurasia 25, 26, 27, 29, 30
Europe 2; Black Death and 57; geography 24; global economic growth and 2; policies of 24; political dominance 24
exclusion test 4
export: floriculture 93; natural resource products 93–94

Factor Endowments Hypothesis 78
factor price equalization 78, 80, 96–97
famines, India 44–45
fertility/fertility rate 59, 92; *see* birth rate
feudalism 26–27; *see also* land transport
Fleming, Alexander 11
floriculture 93
Ford, Henry 17
Franco-Spanish War 61
French haute cuisine and the spice trade 64-65
Fukuyama, Francis 96

Galbraith, Kenneth 86
Gang of Four 81, 83
Gardi, Ibrahim 38
GDP 2, 45, 50–51, 54–55, 69, 70, 79, 87, 93
geography 8–9; technology and 21
Germany 2, 6, 8, 20, 57, 63, 70, 71, 72, 73, 76; economic unification of 73; industrial development of 73
Glorious Revolution of 1688 60
Grand Canal, China 26, 34
Green Revolution 83, 85, 87
Grey, Elisha 11
Griliches, Z. 13

Index **107**

Gulf War 88
Gutenberg, Johannes 8

Haiti 50, 51, 54–55
Hall-Heroult process 11
Han Chinese rulers 29, 33–34
Hastings, Warren 40
Hawkins, John 58
Heckscher, Eli 78
hegemony 1
Henry VIII of Britain 57
Henry the Navigator 35
Hero 10
high-wage economies 97
Hindu rate of growth 87
Hoffman, P. T. 38
Holland *see* Dutch/Dutch Republic
Hong Kong 76, 81

Iberian countries 2
illegal migration 77
immigration 91
import-substituting industrialization (ISI) 84, 87
Inca 49, 50, 61
inclusive growth 55
India 84–88; agriculture 41, 43–45; British government 40–45; budget deficits 87–88; bureaucrats and politicians 85; corruption 85; cotton textiles/textile mills 42–43; distribution of benefits 86; famines 44–45; government employment 86, 87; Green Revolution 85, 87; gunpowder technology 37; Hindu rate of growth 87; import-substituting industrialization (ISI) 84, 87; labour laws 86; Mughal empire 37, 38; per capita GDP 45; policy-making 85–86; public debt 88; public enterprises/sector 86, 87; public investment 87–88; railway system 44, 84, 85; rent-seeking 85; ship-building 43; steel industry 43; tariff rate 86
Indochina 40
Indonesia 13, 20, 40, 76, 81
industrialization: Asia/Asian growth 81–83; care-intensive activities 54; China 39, 76, 83–84; India 42–44, 84, 87; United States 71–73
Industrial Revolution 2, 6, 10, 12, 37, 39, 50, 51, 53, 54, 56, 66–70, 92, 94, 97
innovations 10–21; constraints on 16–19; demand and 14–16; history of 10–11; profitability 13–14; society and 11–12; state and 11–12

institutions 5–6, 54–55
intellectual property rights 17
International Monetary Fund 88
international trade: factor prices 78; neoclassical theory of 78; transport cost and 77–81
Italy 2
Ivory Coast, Asian growth and 93

Jamaica 51, 55
Japan 76
Johnson, S. 3–6, 8, 51, 52, 55
joint stock companies 60
Jungarian corridor 29

Kelly, William 11
knowledge 17; technical 16; *see also* research
Korea 97
Krugman, Paul 77

labour-abundant countries 77–78
labour-intensive goods 78
labour market 98
labour-saving innovation 12, 13–14, 68
Landes, David 40
land transport 24, 25, 26–27, 45, 54, 71, 73
Latin America 52, 53, 81, 92, 93
Lau, Lawrence 7
Logic of Collective Action, The (Olson) 86
Louis XIV of France 12, 36, 65
low-wage economies 97, 98

Malaysia 76, 81
Manchu empire, China 2
man-made restrictions 96
Mansfield, E. 13
Mao 76, 84
marriage 59–60
Marthand Verma and the Battle of Colachel 37–38
mechanization 68
Medieval Warm Period 57
Mediterranean countries 2; *see also* Italy
Merton, Robert 11
Mesoamerica 49
Mexico 49, 50–51, 53, 61
Meyer, Julius Lothar 11
Middle Ages: China (*see* China); European access to sea 30–33; India (*see* India); nomad 28–30, 45–46; Portugal (*see* Portugal); regional balance of power 27–28; transport and economy 25–30; West s domination of Asia 40–45
Middle East 88

108 Index

migration: illegal 77; man-made barriers to 77; restrictions 75, 77, 96
military investment and innovation 18–19
Ming empire, China 2, 26, 30, 31, 33, 34–35, 37, 39, 50, 53
Mongolia 29
Moors 35, 36
Murphy, T. E. 52–53

natural resource products, export of 93–94
Navigation Acts 36, 43, 64
navigation technology 6
neo-Luddite uprising 97
Netherlands *see* Dutch/Dutch Republic
Newcomen, Thomas 10, 13
newly industrializing countries (NIC) 76, 81
New Zealand 3, 39, 71
nomads 28–30, 45–46
Norsemen 57
North America 52, 76, 92

Ohlin, Bertil 78
Olson, Mancur 40, 85
open-ocean navigation 6, 7–8, 66, 71, 75; Britain and 57–59, 64; China and 35; European geography and 23–24; pioneers 7–8; problem of 12; rise of 23, 31; techniques and instruments 8; Western (Atlantic) Europe 46
O Rourke, K. H. 70
Otto, Nicolaus 8, 72
output-based schemes of payment 54

Parker, Geoffrey 38–39
Parthasarathi, Prasannan 45
penicillin 11
personalized services 98
Peru 53
Philip II of Spain 12, 36, 61, 62, 63
Philip III of Spain 62
plague 57; *see also* Black Death
Poland 70, 73
Pomeranz, Kenneth 39
population densities 2
population growth 59–60
Portugal 49, 51, 57, 61, 62, 64; Asian waters 32; Atlantic explorations 24; colonial institution 50; maritime transport 19; open-ocean navigation 7–8, 31, 35–37; population decline in 92; sea routes exploration 14–15
power, regional balance of 27–28
price equalization 96–97
printing press 8
programmable computer 8

protectionism 91
Prussia 73
public debt, India 88

Qing China 37

railways 6, 8, 19; Britain 71; Canada 73; East and South Africa 52; Germany 73; India 41, 44, 45, 84, 85; Russia 73; United States (US) 44, 71
recession 93
regional balance of power 27–28
Rei, Claudia 36
research: military investment 18–19; private 16–17; as a production process 16; state 17–19; threat perceptions 18
research and development (R and D) 89
reversals of fortune 1–2; Acemoglu, Johnson and Robinson (AJR) on 3–6
Ricardo, David 92
Robinson, J. 3–6, 8, 51, 52, 55, 76
robots/robotics 97–98
Royal Charles 64
Russia 2, 6, 8, 19, 29, 57, 66, 71, 73
Rybczynski, Tadeusz 81

scale economies *see* economies of scale
Scherer, F. M. 13
Schmookler, J. 13
Schneider, E. B. 52–53
science and scientific revolution 7
security of property and contracts 5
serfdom 60
settler mortality, during colonial expansion 3–4
Shah, Nadir 37
Shelley, P. B. 1
ship-building, India 43
silver production and trade 49, 50
Singapore 76, 81
slavery/slave labour 5, 50, 52, 53, 54
Smith, Adam 13, 44
Sokoloff, K. L. 51, 52, 53, 54–55
Solow, Robert 7
South Africa, Asian growth and 93
South Korea 76
Spain 5, 7, 8, 12, 24, 31, 35, 36–37, 49, 53, 57–58; battle of Lepanto 61; failure of 61–63; population 62; Thirty Years War 62
spice trade 15
Sri Lanka 20, 34, 37–38, 52
Statute of Monopolies 60
steam engine 10, 11, 67, 68
steel industry, India 43

Index **109**

Stephenson, George 8, 19, 71
Stevens, Nettie 11
Sung empire, China 33–34, 35, 39
Sushruta 10
Sushruta Samhita 10

Taiwan 76, 81, 92
Tatas 43
Taylor, A. M. 70
technical knowledge 16
technology 6–9; future 96–98; innovations
    10–21; transport (*see* transport)
technology of cotton growing 54
technology of sugar cultivation 53–54
telegraph 11
telephone 11
Thailand 76, 81
Third Battle of Panipat 37, 38
Thirty Years War 32, 62, 64, 66
Tipu Sultan 38
trade secrets 17
transport: international trade and 77–81;
    land 24, 25, 26–27, 45, 54, 71, 73; Middle
    Ages 25–30; ocean (*see* open-ocean
    navigation); railways (*see* railways)
Treaty of Westphalia 62
Trump, Donald 90
Turing, Alan 8
Turko-Mongol dynasties 29

United States (US) 2, 3, 5, 6, 8, 19, 43; Civil
    War 72; fertility rate 92; industrialization
    71–73; innovativeness 15; labour-saving
    invention 12; nationalist isolationist

view 90–91; railways 44, 71; research
    and development (R and D) 89; scale
    economies 72–73; wages 12
urbanization 2, 56, 61, 69, 71, 72, 82, 93
US South 54; cotton plantations/textile
    industry 50, 53; geography 51–52;
    mortality rates 51; slavery 52

Verma, Martand 37
Vernon, Raymond 82

wage differentials, demographics and 92
West: comparative advantage 75; decline
    of 88–91; domination of Asia 40–45;
    labour force 89–90; nationalist ideologies
    90–91; research and development
    (R and D) 89; working class and
    Hobson s choice 90
Western Europe 6, 40, 70, 82, 92–93;
    China compared with 39; Industrial
    Revolution (*see* Industrial Revolution);
    institutions 3, 4, 27; nomadic advance
    29; open-ocean navigation 46
Whitney, Eli 50, 68
Wilson, E. B. 11
women 91–92
wood 58, 59
World Bank 92
Wright, Edward 58

Young, Alwyn 7

Zamorano, Rodrigo 58
Zheng He 30, 34–35

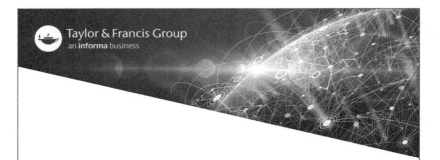